CHAN HEART, CHAN MIND

CHAN HEART,
CHAN MIND

*A Meditation on
Serenity and Growth*

Master Guojun

Edited by Kenneth Wapner

Wisdom

Wisdom Publications
199 Elm Street
Somerville, MA 02144 USA
wisdompubs.org

© 2016 Master Guojun
All rights reserved.

Dongshan poem on page 1 is from *Two Zen Classics* by Katsuki Sekida (New York: Weatherhill, 2000).

Library of Congress Cataloging-in-Publication Data
Guo, Jun, 1974– author.
  [Speeches. Selections. English]
  Chan heart, Chan mind : a meditation on serenity and growth / Master Guojun ; Edited by Kenneth Wapner.
    pages cm
  ISBN 1-61429-262-0 (pbk. : alk. paper)
  1. Religious life—Zen Buddhism. 2. Zen Buddhism—Doctrines. I. Wapner, Kenneth, editor. II. Title.
  BQ9286.2.G86 2016
  294.3'927—dc23

                        2015028489

ISBN 978-1-61429-262-3   ebook ISBN 978-1-61429-289-0

20 19 18 17 16   5 4 3 2 1

Original calligraphy is by Master Guojun. Cover photograph © James Perdue/ EyeEm, GettyImages. Cover design by Laura Shaw Design, Inc. Interior design by Gopa&Ted2, Inc. Set in ITC Galliard Pro 10/16.2.

MIX
Paper from
responsible sources
FSC® C011935

Please visit fscus.org.

TABLE OF CONTENTS

I. *Making Ink*

   1. Making Ink   3

   2. Not No, Non-   13

   3. Grasping   15

   4. "What Is Wu?"   19

   5. The Body Is Just the Body   23

   6. Competition   25

   7. I Breathe, Therefore I Am   27

   8. Effortless Effort, Gateless Gate   31

II. *Steps Along the Way*

   9. "What Is It?"   37

   10. Happiness and Pleasure   41

   11. A First Test   45

   12. Crossing Over   53

   13. Dealing with Sickness   55

   14. Tolerance   57

   15. Faith and Practice   63

   16. Original Nature   67

III. *Chan Heart, Chan Mind*

17. Talking Softly 77
18. Body and Mind Together 79
19. Seeing Beyond the Self 83
20. Courage (II) 87
21. Self-Reliance 91
22. The Nonestablishment of Words 95
23. Tongue of the Buddha 97
24. Repentance 99
25. Loyalty 109
26. Taking For Granted 113
27. Warm Yourself Up! 115
28. All Around Us, All the Time 117
29. Sky Poem (II) 119

IV. *Engaging with the World*

30. Mara's Armies 123
31. Open Heart, Open Mind 127
32. React/Respond 131
33. We Give Meaning to Our Lives 133
34. You've Already Got It! 137
35. Learning to Feel 139
36. Hugging a Monk 141
37. Engaging with the World 145

Acknowledgments   153

Editor's Note   155

About the Author   157

I.

MAKING INK

Long seeking it through others,
I was far from reaching it.
Now I go by myself:
I meet it everywhere.
It is just I myself,
And I am not itself.
Understanding this way,
I can be as I am.

Dongshan

I. MAKING INK

My ordination master, Songnian, was renowned for his calligraphy and considered a National Living Treasure in Singapore.

We Chinese say the way you write tells a lot about who you are. Of Songnian, the man who shaved my head, they used to say, "His writing is without fire." As a young novice I wondered at the cool, flowing quality of his characters; Songnian relentlessly pelted me with fiery insults and rebukes. I had to assume that his art was a window into a facet of his personality that I never saw.

Songnian had come from an aristocratic Chinese family and had been forced to flee the mainland when the Communists seized power in 1949. He drifted to Taiwan, Hong Kong, and Malaysia, eventually settling in Singapore.

When I came to live in his small Mahabodhi Monastery, I was twenty-one years old and he was in his mid-eighties, an old man beset by ailments. Only four nuns lived at Mahabodhi, and they were quietly delighted, almost smirking; as the youngest and most recent arrival, I would be his attendant and bear the brunt of his foul temper.

Mahabodhi was furnished with art and antiques. Money was very tight so I assumed Songnian had bartered for these valuable items with his calligraphy. His strange and lovely bonsais were everywhere. The monastery felt like a scholar's abode, and nowhere was this feeling stronger than by the big wooden table in the living room where he practiced calligraphy.

One day Songnian caught me watching him draw.

"Do you want to learn this?" he asked. There was something slightly sinister in his tone. With such questions, he was always up to no good. But I did want to learn calligraphy, especially from such a revered master.

"Shifu, thank you!" I eagerly replied and bowed. Shifu, an honorific, means "father-teacher." I *always* had to say Shifu first when I addressed him.

Songnian scowled and dismissed me with a wave of his hand. The next day I was surprised when he called me by name as I was slipping past the open door of his study. I stopped, and he peered at me, not saying a word. His bushy eyebrows curled downward on their ends, almost touching the corners of his eyes. He looked like a fierce old owl.

I deferentially entered, and he beckoned me to his side with an irritated, impatient crook of his finger.

"Make ink," he said and poured a pool of water into

the shallow bowl of a traditional Chinese inkstone, a smooth black disc about six inches in diameter.

I took up the inkstick. Sticks are made from compressed charcoal and are ground against the stone to mix with the water and form ink. Their worth is judged by the charcoal's density and the fineness of its grain. Burnt oils, medicinal herbs, precious metals, and glue can be added to the mix, creating subtle shades and aromas that you can detect in the calligraphy for decades.

Songnian put his hand over mine, and began rubbing the stick's nub around the bowl's center in a steady circular motion. It was an intimate gesture, and I was slightly shocked.

After showing me the method, Songnian sent me away. You might imagine that making ink is quick and easy. It's not. You have to endlessly rub around and around. Press too hard and your hands and arms get tired and you won't be able to complete the task. Rub too gently and the ink does not come out.

Finally I had what I considered ink that was not too thick or thin. I knocked on my master's door and set it before him.

"Numbskull!" he said. "Why are you rubbing it so wide? Do you think water is cheap? I have to pay the water bill." My circular motion was apparently too far up the edges of the bowl, which caused the water to quickly evaporate. "Rub on one point." He grabbed my hand and showed me what he wanted: round and round in tight circles in the center of the bowl.

"Let go," he kept telling me as he guided my stiff and nervous hand. "Just follow it." Our hands went round and round. Finally, I was able to feel his internal energy: his rhythm, movement, and degree of force. A transmission occurred. After that, making ink went smoothly.

When I started learning I expected that I would soon be writing characters or at least practicing strokes in the preparation for writing characters. Yet weeks went by, and I was still making ink.

I grew increasingly bitter. Hadn't the old man heard of prepared ink? Bottles of it were sold all over Singapore. He was living in another century. A dinosaur. My hands turned black. I rubbed and rubbed. Small tight circles. Fingers, wrists, and forearms ached.

If the ink was too thick, he scolded me. "Dimwit! Go away. Thin it out. But *no more water*!"

How do you thin ink without water? In later years, I realized you added thinner ink. As a young novice, though, I was completely baffled.

In addition to making ink, I had to master the exacting techniques for washing and drying Songnian's brushes and cutting the rice paper on which he drew. This cutting was particularly harrowing. Each cut had to be absolutely straight with no ragged edges. I learned to crisply fold the paper and draw the knife across the inside seam. The motion had to be fluid and even or the edge frayed.

"Where did you get that ape paper?" asked my master when my results were less than perfect. "You are still a monkey. Go and shave."

The words "paper" and "monkey" have a similar pronunciation in Chinese. Monkey is pronounced "Hou Zi"; calligraphy paper, "Xuan Zi." He was telling me that the loose strands on the edges of the paper made it look hairy. Like an ape. It was an elegant put-down. He managed to be simultaneously clever, poetic, and insulting.

I learned to fold and roll the paper. If I put one wrinkle in the sheets, he screamed at me: "When the paper was with me, it was young! But with you, it's grown old." He spoke in metaphors and riddles.

His tools had to be exactly placed. An inch too far from him and he shouted: "Do you want to tear my ligaments? You torture an old man!"

If I put the paper too close, his words were a burning lash: "Seeds for hell! Why do you put it so near to me! Do you think I'm too old to stretch my arm?"

Often, after finishing work, he was as happy and contented as a child.

"Who drew this?" he asked, looking at me and smiling.

"Shifu!"

"Really? Was it me?"

"Shifu, I think so."

"Wow! It looks so good. Did I do such a thing? How come I didn't know?"

I was speechless.

Today, I realize this was a teaching. Songnian was pointing me toward something, although at the time I had no idea what it was.

A week after leaving Mahabodhi to continue my Buddhist studies in Taiwan, Songnian died. I still had not drawn a single character. Before I left I was making ink, folding and cutting paper, and cleaning and drying brushes. My master must have sensed my frustration: his last instructions to me on the subject of calligraphy were "In writing the most important thing is not writing."

It was over fifteen years before I took up calligraphy again. The intervening period was filled with learning the meditation techniques of Chan and becoming versed in the Buddhist canon. I lived in Taiwan, Korea, Australia, and America. Finally, in my late thirties, I returned to Singapore to rebuild Songnian's monastery and continue his work.

Today, I study calligraphy from a friend of my master's, another old calligrapher who is harsh with his students—although now that I'm the abbot of a monastery he's very nice to me! I've been working hard on my drawing, and I think I've made some progress.

I often think about those early days and the teachings of Songnian. I didn't fully appreciate them at the time, but they've stayed with me. I have come to understand that through making ink Songnian was teaching me in the traditional manner.

I still make ink by hand. The relaxed, firm, circular motion in the center of the bowl reconstitutes our fractured awareness to a single point. Too often, our minds are broken up, scattered about in bits and pieces. Our thoughts wander here and there. Just like my hand that once splashed the ink too high up the sides of the bowl, our minds are often sloppy and unfocused.

In contrast to my bitterness and frustration as a young man, when I make ink today I relish the single-pointed awareness that the process brings. Making ink insists on patience in a world where everything is quick and fast. We are accustomed to expect speed, ease, and comfort. Making ink is about making the effort, letting it come gradually, slowing down.

I feel the paper the way my master did, gauging its texture and carefully dipping and shaping the bamboo brush's tip. Calligraphy paper is delicate. Apply a brush that is too wet and the ink will soak through. Use too much force and the paper abrades or even tears.

Songnian dipped the brush in water, lightly dried it, and sculpted it by wiping it back and forth on a small square of paper he kept for this purpose off to one side. He brought the brush up to his eyes and took it in, connecting to its shape and texture. He dipped the bristles in the ink and swirled them around, assessing their effect on the ink. He stood in a martial stance, one foot forward, knees slightly bent—a stable, balanced posture, poised for forward motion. In fact, among his many accomplishments, Songnian was a martial arts expert. He was a tall man, broad across the shoulders and chest, strong even in old age.

Songnian always paused before he drew. This pause was powerful. He regulated his breath, and I could feel him empty himself. Then he drew in one fluid movement, smoothly moving forward and down over the white sheet.

As a young novice, I longed for such mastery and grace.

Today, when I make ink, cut paper, and wash and dry my brushes, I understand why Songnian insisted on precision in these seemingly mundane details. How are we going to accomplish big things when we can't do small tasks? He was preparing me to shoulder the responsibility of the Dharma and carry on his legacy.

Songnian didn't just teach me to draw—he taught me the *essence* of drawing. The form is always available; it can always be copied. The essence is what needs to be taught, and this was what he transmitted. It was as small and precise as the tip of the brush; as simple and focused as the small circles of the inkstick in the bowl; as fluid and smooth as the cutting of paper; as vast as the universe, the source of creation that pours forth onto the white field of the paper.

Each time I draw I am grateful to be able to stand with one foot forward. I have inherited the bamboo forest, the pine for the charcoal, and the sun's light and warmth that makes the forest grow. I dissolve into the ink, the white sheet of paper, the infinite universe that recreates itself moment by moment, always and forever changing and becoming.

"Who did this?"

I wonder.

Was it me?

Really?

2. NOT NO, NON-

Everything that comes into being depends on everything else. Nothing arises by itself.

In Buddhism, we often talk about "no self." This is a difficult idea to grasp in English. What we mean is that the self as we usually imagine it doesn't really exist. Just as the daffodil is made up of the nutrients it draws from the soil, the energy of sunlight, the water that helps it grow, and the bees that pollinate, so, too, we are made up of the air we breathe, the food we eat, the water we drink, the ancestors who have come before us and made our lives possible.

But does this mean that because the daffodil is comprised of nondaffodil materials it isn't a daffodil? Of course not! And likewise for each of us.

In Chinese the word for "no self" is *wuwo*, but *wu* does not mean "no" in Chinese. It negates rather than defines. It is indefinite. It is not fixed or concrete. *Wu* connotes fluidity, movement, even hope.

The realization of no self is not at all nihilistic. It simply means that the self is something different from what we habitually assume it to be.

In Chan, emptiness is not nothingness. And nothingness is not nothing. We might say "nonthingness" instead. No self might be better expressed as nonself. Not no, non-.

What is the meaning of nonself? Infinity. The downward sweep of Songnian's hand came out of the place from which each breath comes and goes. Where each moment is born and vanishes. A place of nongrasping where there is complete freedom and everything comes together naturally. A lovely Chinese phrase, *xing yun liu shui*, expresses this. It means clouds flowing across the sky, a stream running downhill in spring without hindrance or obstruction, fully functioning, free but still connected, as clouds are connected to the sky and rivers to the earth.

When we realize that, we don't feel terror or despair. On the contrary: to realize that, to *live* it, gives rise to a feeling of potential and possibility. We are no longer bound to the stifling attachment to who we think we are.

Everything changes, including each one of us. We get stuck because we limit ourselves. We do not really open up and become intimate with the world around us.

Not no, non-.

3. GRASPING

When I was in my teens my class took a weeklong field trip by bus from Singapore to the mountainous countryside of northern Malaysia. Imagine our excitement at being on this adventure with our classmates. We boys were in a particularly boisterous mood, outdoing one another to impress the girls. Being mischievous and rather bold, I was one of the ringleaders of the trouble we were always getting into. We snuck out of our rooms after curfew and disappeared as soon as our teachers' heads were turned. Our chaperones had to constantly chase after and threaten us.

Toward the end of the trip we took a tour to see how the Malaysians of the region hunted monkeys. We traveled by coach to an upland forest. Screaming bands of monkeys swung through the trees. We watched as the hunters dug holes in coconuts that were just big enough for the monkeys to insert their paws. The hunters dug and loosened the flesh inside the holes so the meat was fragrant and juicy. Then they put the prepared coconuts on the ground and hid. It didn't take long for the monkeys to investigate. They thrust their paws inside the coconuts and grabbed the flesh. The hunters sprang from their hiding places. The monkeys screamed and headed back for the shelter of the trees. But their paws, full of coconut meat, were too large to draw back out through the holes, and with coconuts attached to their paws, they couldn't climb. The hunters chased them down, netting them and throwing them into cages. Some were probably used for food—monkey brain is considered a delicacy in Malaysia. Others were trained as coconut pickers. Some went to zoos.

As young boys we laughed at the stupidity of the monkeys as they ran around with coconuts stuck to their paws, unable to escape into the shelter of the trees. We thought they were very foolish, very dense. Why couldn't they just let go of the coconut meat and climb to freedom?

We made a great show of inventing insults about the monkeys to impress the girls. I was one of the perpetrators of this behavior. I was already studying Buddhism and internally questioned myself. Why did I make fun of the monkeys? What was driving me? Why did I feel the need to impress my peers and feel superior to the monkeys?

Behind my jeering façade, I pitied the monkeys and was ashamed at the way I egged on my friends. The monkeys screamed in terror. The hunters sprinted after them, hurling their nets. We boys laughed and laughed.

This incident stuck with me as I engaged more deeply with Buddhism. How similar we are to those monkeys! Why can't we just let go? We trap ourselves by our grasping and craving. Why are we so greedy?

Songnian wasn't being stingy when he scolded me about his water bill. We should only use what we need, even if that is an insignificant amount of water. Making ink taught me to use just enough strength when I rubbed, not too much or too little. Just enough. And yet we always want more, more, more!

In order to free itself, the monkey needs to relax. To stop grasping. The same is true for us. Just relax when you see the coconut. Don't be affected or distracted. Let it be. Remind yourself not to be like the monkey. Learn to relax. Whatever happens, relax. Stop grasping. Open your hand.

4. "WHAT IS WU?"

Huatou practice, which is similar but not identical to the Japanese Zen practice of *koan*, has ancient roots in Chinese Buddhism. *Hua* means a sentence; *tou* is "head" or "beginning." The sentence is usually in the form of a question, a seemingly unsolvable riddle.

Huatou gives rise to great inquiry, what Chan calls "great doubt."

The huatou can seem to be meaningless, nonsensical, illogical. The point is not to "solve" a huatou; the point is to use it to investigate. Each time you raise the phrase you go deeper, back to its beginning when the mind starts to move.

The practice is uniquely Chinese in origin, coming from the eleventh century, although the spirit of huatou was always present in Buddhism. Sickness and death, for instance, were the huatou that pushed the Buddha to leave his sheltered life. "What is the source of suffering?" is the huatou to which he kept returning until he finally awakened. It is still a good question—perhaps the best question!

Can you answer it?

Sometimes a question rises from deep in your mind—a

burning question. That is your true question. Where will you find the answer? By using the sentence, you track it down. You find its traces. You keep going back and digging deeper.

There are traditionally many different huatou that people repeat. In our school, Dharma Drum, founded by Master Sheng Yen, we use the huatou "What is Wu?" It has been passed down for many generations and proved to be powerful.

The question originates with Chan Master Zhaozhou (778–897). One of his disciples had been studying the Mahayana Mahaparinirvana Sutra, in which it says that all sentient beings have buddha nature.

The disciple kept a dog to guard the temple. When he read this, he looked at his dog and thought, "My dog has buddha nature!"

Later, when he was serving his master tea, the disciple mentioned that he had read all sentient beings had buddha nature. "So, in this case, my dog has buddha nature, isn't that so?" he said.

"Wu!" Zhaozhou replied.

As we've discussed, *wu* means "non-"—it negates without defining. "Why?" the disciple wondered. The sutra said that all sentient beings have buddha nature! His dog was a sentient being. Therefore his dog should have buddha nature. Why negate that assertion? He was perplexed. What is wu? He kept turning it over and over in his mind, unable to arrive at an answer.

A thousand years later, we are still asking the question. What is wu? We keep asking and asking. We don't ask ourselves, because we have no answer. We just ask and ask. We ask with curiosity. What is wu? What is wu? What is wu?

And wu, believe it or not, has the answer. If you find out the answer of wu, you awaken. But the answer doesn't come from you. It doesn't come from thought or knowledge. We can't figure it out. It is beyond our experience.

Keep asking and asking. Constantly searching. Wanting to discover. What is wu?

Enlightenment is simply seeing our original nature. Seeing reality. Seeing the truth. You attain. You realize. Wu!

You realize what your life is about. Why the world exists. Why there is suffering. Why you were born. Why you were born into one family and not another. Why this country and not that one. You finally know why you are here.

At some point in our lives most of us are intrigued by those mysteries, but we become absorbed with mortgage payments, bringing up the kids, forging careers, and chasing after—what? Success? Fame?

We just go along with what seems to be our lot in

life, what's been handed to us. Everyone was born, so I was born. Everyone goes to school, so I go to school. Everyone graduates, and me too. Everyone looks for a partner; I want one. And so forth, until we retire, travel the world, grow old, and wait for what? Death? We forget to ask, "What is wu?"

Each day, we wake, go to work, finish work, return home, eat dinner, watch TV, sleep, chat on the phone, go to the movies. On the weekend, we sleep late, meet friends, go to a party, take a walk, dine out. Day after day. Week after week. Month after month. Year after year.

Why? Why are we doing all this? What is happening? Who are we?

"Oh," you might respond. "I'm a lawyer, father, manager, millionaire, Chan master, writer, son, daughter, uncle, astronaut, athlete, teacher, Jain, Jew, Buddhist!"

What if all that is taken away from you? Then who are you? What is your true identity other than these things? Do you ever wonder who you really are? Do you want to find out?

Wu!

What is wu?

5.   THE BODY IS JUST THE BODY

We live inside our bodies, and we identify with them. When we experience itchiness, we say, "I'm itchy." If there's pain, we're generally miserable and think to ourselves, "Woe is me. I'm in pain!"

If we look more deeply, we see that "we" don't experience pain. Our bodies do.

A mosquito stings you. You say, "The mosquito bit me!" In fact, the mosquito did not bite *you*; the mosquito bit your nose or somewhere else on your body.

Shift your awareness. Separate your identification of the body with the self. You will have less attachment to the body, and whatever happens to the body will be less affecting. When you look at the mirror you won't scream because of one more white hair or wrinkle. The body ages, but it's not *you* that has aged. You won't moan and groan about every little ache and pain. Your body is experiencing some discomfort. *You* don't have to be uncomfortable. Everything changes, including your physical state. Be patient. Relax. Give it time.

The body is just the body. Overly identifying with it limits us. It stunts our growth and makes us claustrophobically self-involved. It separates us from the rest of creation. It makes us selfish and fearful, and it cuts us off from true intimacy and connection.

6. COMPETITION

We learn to compete from an early age. Our parents instill the idea that we should do well each day, trying to prepare us for the competition we will inevitably face.

In school we compete against our peers for the best grades, for the approval of our teachers, and in sports. Who can run the fastest? Make the most goals? Hit the ball the furthest? We compete against rivals to win our sweethearts. After we graduate we compete against our colleagues for promotions, for the largest salary, for the nicest office, for awards and recognition. As we mature, we compete against aging. We compete against sickness. We compete against death. It is never-ending!

To grow we need to stop competing—with others, with ourselves, with time, with the expectation of the way life should go, with our sense of attainment or nonattainment, with wanting this experience or that experience— with everything! We need to see our competitive streak for what it is, recognize it, and let it go.

Songnian wasn't making art; he was living art. It came from deep within him. He wasn't affected by what anyone else was doing. He didn't need to think about whether to do this or that, to make this kind of drawing or that kind of drawing. It was effortless and natural. There was no sense of "me" against "them," no need to push, force, or exert. Songnian's energy was smooth and steady. He had attained a natural mastery and was simply expressing what was inside of him.

What's inside of you doesn't really have to do with anyone else. But it's a gift to all of us.

7. I BREATHE, THEREFORE I AM

When you do calligraphy, you move slowly. Your breath slows. Songnian would take one deep breath and draw. After he finished, he would relax. His breath would be long and deep.

Our breath expresses who we are. When we change the way we breathe, we change our lives.

Tu na is qigong practice. *Tu* means exhale, expel, discharge, subtract, eliminate, release, and exclude. *Na* means to inhale, receive, take in, assimilate, rejuvenate, and recharge.

Chan took up these energetic exercises of regulating the body and breath and developed them into spiritual practices that are not only about the individual but how we connect with each other and the world.

If we quarrel, the breath inside our bodies become stale. We don't fully release. The breath tightens. This is the way we hold on to hurt. How do we let go? Loosen the breath. Discharge emotionally and psychologically.

Exhale. Breathe out. Breathe it out. Breathe it all the way out.

———

We're afraid to deeply breathe. *Na* means to open up. To receive. We're afraid of change. We shut ourselves off from learning. When our breath deepens and slows, our understanding deepens. We have a bigger heart.

In a tense and nervous state, our breath is shallow. It occurs only in our chests. The inhale is rushed, half-hearted, shallow. When we're impatient, our breath becomes short.

In a relaxed state, we breathe deeply. We fill our lungs. It's so natural, so true.

When we see a very beautiful scene in nature, our breath is full of wonder, and we sigh.

When we're deep in thought, before an important decision or task, we take a deep breath and then go ahead.

Talking to a friend and sharing something important, we breathe deeply. Our breath slows.

When we take our time, our breath slows.
When we're shortsighted, our breath is shallow.
When we feel deeply,
Our breath deepens.

The breath is a manifestation of our inner state. Our character is reflected in our breath.

———

Each breath is different. Every breath. Take in new air; fill up your lungs with new breath. Let go on the out breath. Empty yourself. Discharge. Release. Expel.

Relax the breath and you relax yourself. This is how we learn and grow. Each breath is delicious, each breath is an affirmation. Savor each breath. Breathe deep and long and slow.

8. EFFORTLESS EFFORT, GATELESS GATE

When Songnian first taught me to grind the inkstick, he was preparing me to hold a brush. You hold the stick to make ink in the same way you hold the brush to write. Both the shaft of the stick and the brush face downward at a right angle: only their tips touch paper or bowl.

Watching the way Songnian held the brush was mesmerizing. This grip is called *xuquan*, the hollow fist. His wrist was loose and drooped. Long fingers extended down the brush shaft. The graceful motion of his hand was so refined—the embodiment of Chinese art and culture!

I have learned to hold the brush as Songnian did, in the hollow fist. The hollow represents holding but not holding, what Chan calls effortless effort, the gateless gate. My grip is gentle but firm, as if I were securely cradling an egg.

Holding and gripping are different. Gripping is tense and forceful. Holding is flexible, fluid, and adaptable. The straight shaft of the brush can rotate a full 360 degrees. It is like the *enso*, the Zen circle without beginning or end. The gateless gate, through which we enter Chan, has no fixed point of entry. No fixed gate.

Songnian would begin his work from all points on the paper. He had mastered effortless effort. It flowed from the way he held the brush.

They say that when a tiger approaches, everything in the forest suddenly becomes completely still. There is a sense of presence, of imminence. And yet you may never see the tiger. As a young novice I could feel what I imagine is a similar atmosphere in the pause before Songnian drew: that same stillness, that same feeling of presence and power. In Chan, this is emptiness.

Songnian was always following me with his sharp eyes as I went about my tasks. I could walk in front of him once, and he would just stare at me. But if I walked twice, he would rebuke me: "Lazy cat!" (I was born in the year of the tiger.) "Why are you so idle? What a shiftless dolt you are! Go and scrub my bathroom floor." He seemed to enjoy making me stop and attend to him when I was particularly busy. Sometimes I suspected that he would decide to do calligraphy when he knew I had a lot of work out of spite. "Set up the table and put things in order," he commanded. I had to drop whatever I was doing, make ink, and set out his paper and tools.

The laying out of his implements was an ongoing saga: there was no set way he wanted them placed. One day his brushes were on the left; the next, on the right. Sometimes they were below the paper; sometimes above.

There was no fixed or definite pattern. It was the method of no method, effortless effort, the gateless gate.

Early on in my apprenticeship, I put the brushes in the position that they had been set out the last time he had drawn. I would invariably be scolded and told to rearrange them.

After several tongue-lashings, I thought I could outfox him. "Shifu, brushes left or right?" I asked the next time he told me to arrange the table.

"What do you think?" he replied. I was left to guess. And of course my arrangement displeased him.

"Stupid cat!" he said and left it at that.

The next time, I asked him again: on the left or right? "Left," he replied.

I couldn't believe my good fortune. I placed the tools on the left.

Again I was scolded. "Wrong side," he hissed. "Your left side is not my left side!"

The next time I asked, "Shifu! Your left or my left?"

"Which 'left' do you think?" he said, peering at me. I could only guess, and, of course, I was scolded.

The next day, I asked him again. This time he didn't say anything—he just peered at me.

When I asked yet again, he said "No left!" Then he ignored me.

It was a maddening game. The deck was stacked: I could never win.

I actually use this same approach today with my students to point to the relative nature of appearances. My left is not your left. If I tell you to point to the left side of the room, will you point to your left or my left? Where is left? Your left is my right and so forth. Reality based on the perspective of subject and object is always relative. Songnian conveyed that fundamental Buddhist teaching to me in his own way.

It takes time to learn how to create the hollow fist. The hollow must be gentle; you cannot force it. Gentleness gives space to others because it doesn't impose and push its way. It allows you to be you and me to be me. Without sufficient space, there is friction.

Holding and gripping are very different. Try to find the gate and it's gone. It's everywhere and nowhere. Any point is the entry point.

When I miss Songnian, I prepare the table. I lay out my brushes. I make ink. I slow down. I hold the brush in the hollow fist. I don't grip or grasp. I cradle the egg. I stand with one foot forward. I pause. Take a long deep breath. And then I draw.

II.

STEPS ALONG THE WAY

Gateless is the ultimate way:
There are thousands of ways to it.
If you pass through this barrier,
You may walk freely in the universe.

Master Wumen,
from The Gateless Gate

9. "WHAT IS IT?"

In 1999, when I was in my mid-twenties, I did a special retreat practice in Korea—three hundred thousand prostrations in one hundred days. My health was not good, but I persevered; I was determined to practice.

I'd been moving from monastery to monastery for stretches of a week to a month when I came to Bae Yang Sa, or "White Goat Monastery." I wanted to meet an old monk there. He was famous for always asking, "*Yimoko?*" which translates as "What is it?" or "What is this?" Yimoko was his huatou practice.

Bae Yang Sa was in a remote southwestern part of the Korean peninsula. It was fall, and the weather was turning colder. I traveled by train, bus, then on foot. My journey took me on quiet roads, along rivers, through beautiful forests.

I arrived at the monastery, went to the office, put down my bags, and prostrated myself to the person in charge. I told him where I was from and why I had come. I was shown to an empty room, 7 x 7 feet, with a thin mattress, small pillow, and blanket.

That afternoon I was brought to meet the old monk.

Given his impact on my life and practice, I'm ashamed to say that I've forgotten his name.

He sat in a room with only one chair, like a throne. His attendant sat on the floor beside him. I knelt on a large rectangular brown cushion. The old monk's robes were gray, as is customary in Korea.

Perhaps because the monastery was called White Goat, to my young eyes he looked like an old goat of the mountain. Although his face and head were clean-shaven, I saw a white goat-like beard and horns curling up around his ears, and I had an impression of great stability and stillness. I imagined a white goat on high gray cliffs who traversed perilous terrain with surefooted ease. He gazed at me, and his eyes did not flicker or move.

The old monk asked about my practice. I told him about my experience with the breath and also my experience with huatou. I explained that I had been dissolving into the breath, forgetting my body and time and space. I became the breath, and I felt open and spacious.

When I investigated huatou, there was a pressing need to *know*. I was using the huatou "What is your original nature before you were born?" and I had been wondering about this question for a very long time. Where had I come from? Why was I who I was and not someone else? I would forget myself as I pressed into this question. There was only this one question, and it became one sound. That sound echoed through the mountains, reverberating in the vast universe.

I said I felt lost, as though I were a wandering child. I was an orphan, longing for my lost parents. I longed to go home. I pressed in on the huatou. I wondered: what did I really look like? What was my original face? The mirror couldn't—or wouldn't—show it to me. The face I saw there was not the face I longed to see. The face that I touched with my hands was an imposter, the face of someone else; I didn't even know if it belonged to me. It was the face of someone named Guojun. Was that who I was? It was a meaningless face, a pale facsimile. I longed to see my original face. I was lost, an orphan. I was wandering, and my wandering had brought me here.

The old monk was very still, quietly listening. We spoke in Korean; when I couldn't understand him or he couldn't understand me his attendant interceded. I would write my ideas out in Chinese characters and the attendant would read what I had written to the White Goat in Korean.

When I had finished telling him all this, he said, "Good. Continue on with your practice." Then he invited me for tea. On a thick slab of wood next to him on the floor, the attendant made green tea with toasted grains of rice. Its fragrance filled the room. I took the cup between my palms: steam enveloped my face. I breathed it in and felt warm.

After we had finished with tea, the White Goat told me to ask of everything that I saw, heard, tasted, or touched, "What is it?" He asked me to go beyond form, beyond appearances. "What is all this?" he asked. There was a long silence. I was very touched. I experienced a kind of opening, and I prostrated. The old monk smiled. That was the second time he had smiled. The first was when I told him about my experiences with the practice. He smiled and slowly nodded his head like an old goat quietly chewing on grass. I finished my tea and left. When I opened the door to his quarters, I saw the sky—vast and open.

The sun went down, and I joined in the evening service, participating when I could. There were many unfamiliar pieces of liturgy, but I could follow along when they chanted the Heart Sutra. Its opening message— form is emptiness and emptiness is form—had a special resonance for me that night.

When I left White Goat, I walked many miles through the mountains, through the vast forests, asking myself over and over, "What is it?" "What is it?"

The old monk's eyes stayed with me.

Very still.

Very calm.

10. HAPPINESS AND PLEASURE

Happiness and pleasure are often confused, although they have different qualities. Pleasure is short-lived. It's not sustainable; it doesn't fulfill us. It's empty of true substance or nourishment.

Eating good food can bring you pleasure. If you're hungry, this enjoyable experience can seem to be the same as happiness. But you can't keep eating and eating; if I force-fed you after you were full, what would you feel?

Pleasure is ephemeral. It comes with a limited capacity and an inevitable saturation point. During my mandatory military service in Singapore, I counseled addicts. They described the intense, transient pleasure they got from drugs. When they came down, they felt hollow and desperate.

It's the same with all our appetites, the things that give us pleasure. When you're itchy, you scratch, but the scratching doesn't get rid of the itch; it just replaces one sensation with another. We always want the quick, easy way out. Pleasure does not give us complete and total satisfaction, yet we constantly chase it. Why?

Perhaps because we have an underlying sense of fear.

These states are simply other kinds of distractions from our fundamental existential discomfort. We feel, unconsciously, that something is missing. We rarely feel completely whole, and yet we crave wholeness. We're afraid of our own mortality and insignificance.

Admitting this is terribly hard for us, so we develop defense mechanisms: One more potato chip. Another chocolate bar. Another drink or joint. We bury and camouflage this part of ourselves, chasing after things that do not really satisfy us.

Looking at what is fearful, insecure, and dissatisfied at our core can be a painful process. We don't want to look, but it's a necessary step if we want to grow.

Instead of always chasing after pleasure, we would feel much more satisfied if we cultivated joy. Pleasure is just physical stimulation, but joy is something more mental and fulfilling. Pleasure is all about me and my selfish sensations; joy comes from embracing what is—and from gratitude.

I've always wondered why we crave pleasure when it's so obviously ephemeral. Why do we chase after ownership and material possessions when the satisfaction they bring is so fleeting?

Even as a young man I knew happiness must be elsewhere—this is what pushed me toward becoming a monk. It led me to Chan, and it's why I kept asking, "What is my original nature?" "Who am I?" "What is it?"

I kept digging and asking and returning to these questions over and over. I wanted something more lasting and stable than pleasure. I wanted to find true happiness.

II. A FIRST TEST

There is a long tradition of Chan masters testing their students. When they do, they don't look for cleverness or erudition. They peer into your heart and mind and gauge the quality of your direct, individual experience.

So it was with my lineage master Sheng Yen. He was a towering figure in Asia, a renowned scholar and practitioner of the Way, an awakened savant who had a huge center in Taiwan and a following of over a million people.

Sheng Yen first tested me in 2002, profoundly altering the course of my life. I had been studying for my bachelor's degree in psychology and sociology in Australia. One of my supporters suggested that I go to New York to meet Sheng Yen; he had a small center in Queens and a place where he held retreats about two hours north of the city in Pine Bush. Although I was busy, I jumped at the opportunity to spend time with this revered master.

I had met Sheng Yen once before, briefly, in Taiwan when I was helping to prepare a memorial book for Songnian, and I asked Sheng Yen to contribute. Both he and Songnian had studied under the same teacher, Dongchu, and they knew one another.

It was a brief meeting; Sheng Yen was notoriously busy. His sharp eyes ran over me, up and down. I felt as if I were being scanned. I could see that he was as thin as a twig under his robes. The impression of frailty was belied by his vigor and the lightness of his step.

"How can I help you?" he asked. I told him what I was doing, and he apologized, saying that he didn't know Songnian well enough to write an article about him. I asked for a few words. He thought for a moment and wrote *Shuhua Sanmei*, which translates as "Calligraphy Samadhi."

"What are you doing now that your master is gone?" he gently asked.

I replied that I was enrolled at the Fu Yan Buddhist Institute in Taipei. He asked about my studies and encouraged me not to give up. I could tell he adored people who liked to learn. I prostrated to him, and he smiled, looked at me in a fatherly manner, and gave me his blessing.

I could see his silhouette through the window as I left. The sun was setting: he was a gaunt black figure. That image has stayed with me.

I returned to the Institute. It was 1998, and it would be several years before I met Sheng Yen again.

After an interminable flight from Australia, I arrived at JFK airport, disoriented and jet-lagged. I was shocked at the way I was treated. I had been in Australia for three years where things were mellow and easy. But this was the United States soon after 9/11, and security was tight. I was subjected to a long, aggressive round of questions and searched.

As I made my way to the airport cabstand, I was stunned by the city's diversity and pace. I gave the cabbie the Queens center's address and arrived shortly before the evening service. It surprised me that Sheng Yen was operating from a humble tenement in an out-of-the-way neighborhood.

After the service, I prostrated before Sheng Yen. When I rose he just looked at me—a long penetrating stare. Then he turned without a word and walked away.

I was shown to my quarters on the second floor in a storage room next to the toilet. There were people sleeping on mats everywhere. A retreat was beginning that weekend and would continue through the coming week. I felt quiet, shy, and glad to finally lie down after the long flight.

We woke at 4:00 a.m., exercised, meditated, and then went to the Chan hall for morning service. Everyone walked softly. The rooms were dim. Only a few lights had been lit here and there.

After a short break that followed the service, we quietly moved to the dining room in the temple's windowless basement for breakfast. I was seated near Sheng Yen.

There was silence during the meal until Sheng Yen spoke. I was shocked—he addressed me! "Why did you become a monk?" he asked.

He looked at me again with the same penetrating gaze with which he had scrutinized me the night before. It was clear that I was undergoing some sort of examination, but I had no idea why.

I would usually have been shy and reserved when talking to someone I did not know well, especially someone with such a huge reputation. But no one had ever asked me that question, at least no one who was actually, *deeply* asking. The floodgates mysteriously opened.

A room full of monks and nuns was listening, but I talked only to Sheng Yen. It was as though he had created an invisible force field around us. He was totally attentive and engaged, and I was at ease, which was peculiar given the situation.

I explained that I had originally wanted to go to medical school but became disillusioned with my fellow premed students who seemed more interested in status and money than helping people. I had been offered a scholarship to the Polytechnic Institute in Singapore to study biotechnology. Genetics particularly interested me. I wanted to understand how the brain functioned and why we're all so different.

But I soon found that while it seemed that science could often explain *how* things worked, it wasn't able to provide a reason for *why*. I joined different religious clubs for students at the Polytechnic. I tried Catholicism, Islam, and then Buddhism. When I heard Buddhist teachings of no self, cause and effect, and dependent co-origination, a giant gong echoed inside me.

"Hmmm," said Sheng Yen, nodding and smiling. He indicated that I should proceed.

I found myself telling him about my childhood, when the idea of becoming a doctor had first occurred to me. I was six, and my grandfather had passed away. He lived in the Lim Chu Kang area of Singapore, which at that time was farmed (now it's covered with high rises and served by a subway). Getting there involved a long bus ride and a walk along hot, dusty roads that cut through mangrove swamps swarming with mosquitoes and biting flies. The adults talked in *Teochew* dialect, which I barely understood. For someone who fancied himself a cosmopolitan child from the big city, the whole experience was an irksome ordeal. It all felt very backward and provincial, a nightmare for a young boy who would rather have been at home, swimming in the neighborhood pool or watching kung fu movies and playing video games.

We stayed at my grandparent's farm for days as my relatives mourned and my grandfather lay in his burial robe in a black coffin. Incense smoke clouded the room. Mosquitoes buzzed in the still, hot air. It was depressing and spooky for a young child.

This was my first experience of death. No one could explain why such a terrible thing had happened.

Compounding my grandfather's death was the death from tuberculosis soon after of my grandma, my mother's mother, who was like a best friend to me. She began coughing blood, had to be hospitalized, and wasted away. No one could help her. I resolved to become a doctor and learn to conquer illness so my mother and father would not fall sick and leave me.

At the Polytechnic I realized medicine had no answer to death. It was useful but limited. That was another important reason that I had turned to religion.

"Hmmm," Master Sheng Yen said, smiling and nodding. "Go on. Tell me everything."

I recounted my time in the basic military training required of all young people in Singapore. I was posted to a counseling service in drug rehabilitation. I don't know why they chose me for this enviable position, but I didn't have to wear a uniform and was allowed to return home each evening.

The suffering of addicts affected me. Some came from wealthy families and had grown up with every advantage, yet they were desperate and miserable. I clearly saw that the physical body is not the source of happiness. I felt compassion for them, and I wanted to serve; I wanted to grapple with the basic problems of living. I was inspired by the compassion of the Buddha. He had walked away from riches and power. That moved me, and I was drawn to the idea of becoming a monk.

"Very good," said Sheng Yen. With that he got up from the table and left me sitting there, wondering what had come over me to embark on such a long explanation.

I felt as though I had emptied myself. I was relieved and relaxed. And, subtly, I had a deeper understanding of my motives and the arc of my life. Although I didn't realize it at the time, my teacher had started teaching me, guiding my steps along the way, preparing me to go deeper.

After I got to know Sheng Yen, I asked him to name the stupa I had built for Songnian's memorial in 2004, eight years after Songnian had passed away. The name, written on a piece of paper, would be scanned and then engraved by laser on a black marble slab that would stand next to the stupa.

Before setting pen to paper, Sheng Yen hesitated for a long time.

"Songnian is so famous! My calligraphy is unworthy," he said. He finally produced several versions of "Grandmaster Songnian, calligrapher," and he asked, a little shyly, which version I preferred.

In his hesitation and feelings of inadequacy I saw Sheng Yen's humility. He was one of the most revered Buddhist masters of his generation, but like the hollow bamboo, he was empty of schemes or ulterior motives. The taller the bamboo, the more it bends. Sheng Yen was free of airs. There was a simplicity and innocence about him that is very Chan. His was a lovely, graceful maturity.

Deeply moved, I picked out one of the inscriptions he had drawn for the stupa.

12. CROSSING OVER

Two brothers left home together to look for meditation teachers. At a river near their home they parted ways, vowing to meet again in ten years at the same spot and share what they'd learned.

Both were as good as their word. Ten years passed, and they stood face to face on the riverbank.

"What did you learn?" asked the elder brother.

"Let me show you," said the younger. He sprang into the sky and with a great leap he landed on the far side of the river.

"Come over and join me," he called, pleased with himself. The elder brother hired a *sampan* to ferry him across the river.

The younger brother laughed as the elder disembarked. "What have you learned from your meditation? You can't even jump across this river."

The elder brother smiled. "Is that all you have you learned in these ten years? To jump across a river?"

"I have learned special powers," the younger brother boasted. "I am able to jump great distances and even fly!"

"What you have learned in ten years is only worth two dollars," the elder brother said.

"Why only two dollars?" The younger brother was perplexed.

"That is the cost to cross the river by boat. In my ten years of practice I didn't learn to jump from one riverbank to the other. I learned to cross from the vexations in my mind to the shore of serenity and freedom."

There actually is no other shore. To go beyond the furthest shore is to come back to yourself. When you cross over, you stand in the same place you're standing now. All our journeys bring us back to where we began.

We often think true spirituality is ethereal, mystical, extraordinary, even supernatural! And yet it is this present moment that is most extraordinary. It brims with mystery, possibility, and hope.

13. DEALING WITH SICKNESS

We get sick. That's life! It is the rare person who never falls ill. Most of us are prey to various bugs and infections and a body that is as imperfect as everything else in the world.

The Buddha said that caring for the sick brings the greatest merit. He cared for them himself, washing his ailing followers and soothing their spirits with teachings about impermanence and nonattachment to the body. Sometimes after hearing these teachings his disciples miraculously became well.

Stories of miraculous recovery were on my mind when I became quite ill a few days before I was due to lead a ten-day meditation retreat in Indonesia. The illness began in the morning. By midafternoon I had severe cramping and diarrhea. I had to dash to the toilet every fifteen minutes. I couldn't sleep at night and moved the living room couch outside the bathroom so that the toilet was close by.

Through three long nights I meditated on what it must be like to give birth and undergo the intense spasms of labor. I felt gratitude for what my mother had endured to bring me into the world.

After the fourth day, things got a bit better, although I was still cramping and dehydrated and very weak. I had to run the retreat, give talks, sit in meditation, and lead morning and evening service. I thought I'd have to do all this in diapers!

Fortunately, that turned out not to be the case. When I performed my duties, I put my attention on what I was doing, and I forgot the diarrhea. But the moment I was done, I cramped and had to run to the bathroom.

Those ten days were very tough. The only thing I could do was relax. I surrendered myself to the sickness. I learned to live with it. I remembered the Buddha's words about nonattachment and impermanence. I can't say I was miraculously cured, although these teachings did make me realize that I had a choice—to be upset about my condition or relax.

Each breath is a good breath. Every day is a good day. Every moment is a good moment. We can always learn and grow.

At the end of the retreat, the day after it was finished, the illness passed.

14. TOLERANCE

The capacity for tolerance, acceptance, is an important part of learning and growing in the Chan tradition. Tolerance in Chan is not about gritting your teeth and bearing it; it's about being totally at ease and peaceful even while experiencing pain—even in the presence of death.

When we have tolerance, we are relaxed. Without tolerance, we're tense and closed. We become less aware. We're not so clear. We don't know how to respond properly, and we have less flexibility.

Our deep, perhaps unconscious longing is to fearlessly enter the flow of life, wherever it takes us. With perfect tolerance, we fully function, completely inhabiting our lives no matter what the circumstances.

Great meditation masters exemplify this kind of tolerance. Master Hsing Yun, president of the Buddha Light Association, is one such example. He teaches "engaged" Buddhism: doing good works, helping people, sponsoring social activities, setting up universities. He is quite old now and almost blind, but you would never know it.

He particularly impressed me when he was greeting people for the second World Buddhist Forum in 2009 at the arrival gate of Taoyuan Airport in Taipei, Taiwan. He had a broken rib, and it was extremely painful for him to stand. Yet he was busy all day, shaking hands and smiling warmly and happily as he greeted thousands of laypeople and monastics at the arrival area to the conference. He stood for the whole day and welcomed each and every person.

What tolerance he had! He's a big man, and there's a majesty about him, like an emperor. He was totally at ease and peaceful, even while he was experiencing what must have been excruciating pain. He inspired me. And his example gave me strength for the Path.

Sheng Yen was another example of this kind of tolerance. Toward the end of his life he went for chemotherapy between his talks to treat the cancer that would eventually take his life. Yet on stage he was like a lion.

I couldn't believe his capacity for tolerance when I was his attendant in 2004. He spent three months in Taiwan, teaching and running his monasteries and Buddhist institutes. Then he took off on a breakneck tour to Singapore, Sydney, Melbourne, and Switzerland. He was teaching in each place, giving talks, and leading retreats. Wherever he went he was constantly making notes in tiny handwriting in a pocket notebook. He noted details of everything he saw, and ideas constantly came to him for the books he was always writing. When

I went to bed, he would still be awake, way past midnight, writing.

He never had jet lag. None whatsoever. I couldn't believe it. Here I was, a young man, and yet by the time I went with him to New York I was a wreck, so sick I almost had to be hospitalized!

Sheng Yen always said to me that his life was limited. He didn't have much time left, and he wanted to make full use of what remained. During this period his blood pressure was irregular and his heartbeat erratic. He was prone to fainting. He was already experiencing kidney failure and had been diagnosed with cancer, but nothing stopped him.

He told me later that he had confided in me about his medical condition only to persuade me to become abbot of his Pine Bush retreat center. In those days the seriousness of his condition was closely guarded. He had yet to make it public.

When he could be more open about his medical issues he seemed to enjoy discussing them. It was as if he were talking about another person. His cancer didn't rattle him or make him anxious or depressed. Hearing him describe his kidney failure was like listening to a class in biology or physiology. He would give a Dharma talk in the morning, go for dialysis in the afternoon, and then give another Dharma talk in the evening. Afterward he didn't even have the strength to talk or lift his hand. Yet he always had the energy to deal with all the problems and challenges involved with running a global organization. His mind was always sharp and clear. What remarkable strength he had!

There is another example of this kind of tolerance that touched me deeply. As a young monk, I went with a group of Buddhists to visit an old man dying of liver cancer in Singapore General Hospital who had been a devout Buddhist for many years.

He'd had a hard life. When he was young, his wife had left him. His business failed. He wasn't well educated and had to work as a laborer. He turned to Buddhism and took up the practice of reciting the name of Amitabha Buddha, which carries the hope that one will be reborn in the Pure Land, the Western Paradise that is similar to the idea of heaven in Christianity.

He was in a ward with six beds. We went to see him in the afternoon. He raised his bed to a half-sitting position to talk to us. There was an astonishing serenity in his face, an absolute sense of peace. There was no fear in him and no expression of pain. This was extraordinary because throughout the course of the illness he had steadfastly refused pain medication.

His doctor was amazed. He had treated cancer patients for almost sixty years, and this was the first time he had seen someone go through radiation, chemotherapy, and the ravages of the disease and still remain totally calm and relaxed, all without medication.

One week after we visited him, the old man died.

When you're sick, it's not you that's sick; it's your body. The mind can choose not to be sick. Being at peace does not necessarily mean that you're comfortable. Part of spiritual growth is developing tolerance.

How many people can die beautifully? Is this worth thinking about and preparing for? I'll leave that up to you.

15. FAITH AND PRACTICE

Strong faith is a form of sincerity.

Faith opens your heart. It gives you strength and courage, and it energizes and motivates you. This faith is not blind faith, however; it involves touching and experiencing.

This kind of faith is a vibration and resonance. It's like a mother and child: When she carries the child inside her body, the mother can feel the baby move, and after the child is born, she remains in tune with him or her. There is a Chinese saying—the cut on the skin of the child is like a cut in the heart of a parent.

The love a mother has for her child is unique, but it's also universal. Faith is like that; it's as though a choir is singing with individual voices in beautiful harmony together. A song of love and kindness.

In Chan, faith comes from practice. In my own case, after I started to learn from Sheng Yen, I had two experiences of meditative absorption that awakened my faith in the teachings. I was living at the retreat center in Pine Bush, helping to lead retreats, but I had not yet taken on administrative responsibilities.

My sitting practice was challenging during this period. I had devoted myself to sitting meditation for years and logged countless hours on the cushion, so you'd think I'd have had it down pat. This, sadly, was not the case. I was experiencing pain in my legs, and I felt as though I were being eaten alive by wandering and scattered thoughts. I was so drowsy that I wondered if I had some kind of wasting disease. Although there had been periods during my practice when my experiences had been quite deep, that summer it seemed as though those days were gone forever.

My first experience of faith occurred when the center was quiet. It was after lunch, and I was alone. The clock in the living room of the sangha house read 2:00 p.m. It was summer, but the room was cool.

I was doing sitting and I experiencing my usual problems: wandering and scattered thoughts, mind-numbing exhaustion. I kept coming back to the breath, returning to the method. Suddenly, there was a shift. I forgot my body and where I was. I forgot who I was and my wandering and scattered thoughts. Everything dropped off. There was a feeling of absolute clarity and calm. I felt as though I were the only person in the whole world. I was an unshakable mountain and at the same time a light feather drifting slowly down through layer upon layer of incense smoke in a perfectly still room.

When I opened my eyes, I thought my vision was impaired. The clock read 8:00 p.m. It seemed inconceivable that I had sat for six hours without being aware of time passing. It was as though time had imploded, evaporating into nothingness.

A similar experience recurred a week later. I was doing walking meditation back and forth across the living room of the sangha house. The room was perhaps four meters in length, and I traversed it slowly, placing each foot down, feeling each joint. My toes touched the floor first, then the ball of my foot, the center of my foot, and finally the heel. I kept returning to the practice, relaxing and resting in the method. I became completely absorbed, and I had the same experience of falling away. When I looked at my watch, four hours had passed, and I had only moved two meters.

The experience of absorption gave me a certain form of nonattachment, a taste of liberation, freedom, cessation from attachment to the self and its attendant suffering. I experienced hope that I might be able to attain liberation. And this gave me faith in the practice and the path.

These types of experiences are shared by all the contemplative traditions of the world. They all have a similarity about them, yet each has its own distinct context and character. They all feel unshakable and true, and they all point us toward liberation and peace, love and kindness— the common language of all spirituality.

16. ORIGINAL NATURE

One day at morning assembly, when I was a young student at Taiwan's Fu Yan Buddhist Institute, it was announced that renowned Dharma master Renjun was coming to teach.

We young monks anticipated Renjun's arrival with a combination of curiosity and dread. His reputation preceded him. He had a Chinese nickname that translated into English as something like "Hair Stands on End" or "Shiver Down the Spine."

Renjun arrived by car on a cold day. He was a short man with the thick glasses of a scholar. His head was shaped like an inverted pear and tilted to one side as though he had a permanent crick in his neck. He had been born in Jiangsu Province on the mainland and spoke with an almost incomprehensible accent. A woman interpreter accompanied him. When she was slow to render his words, or garbled them, he bellowed at her with the manner of an imperious general accustomed to being instantly obeyed.

Most of the young monks scattered like birds at the sound of a gun when they saw him coming; none of them wanted to be his attendant. I volunteered. I thought it would be good training, and my ordination master, Songnian, had recently died. He had been another fierce, exacting old monk, and I missed him.

I brought food to Master Renjun, keeping some in reserve off to the side in case I was rebuked for giving him too small a portion. In the evening, it was my job to bring him a pail of warm water in which to wash his feet. I knocked on his door.

"Come," he said.

I entered bent forward at the waist, my head bowed.

"Can I help you?" I asked.

"No, I'm okay," he replied, proceeding to wash his feet himself, a practice which improves circulation and promotes sleep. I stood by, in my most deferential and unobtrusive posture.

The first night I did this, I adjusted the temperature of the soaking pail with an extra pitcher of hot water I had brought along. When he indicated that the temperature was exactly right, I tested the water with my hand, and from then on I knew exactly how warm he liked it. He must have appreciated my good service because I was never scolded.

Each day, Renjun did sitting meditation in a chair. Then he exercised vigorously, punching up, down, forward, and sideways. To see this funny little man with a crick in his neck punching the air was rather comical to my young eyes. Needless to say, I kept my laughter to myself. Even his prostrations had a martial air: they were quick, rigid, exact.

Part of my job as his attendant was to fetch him when it was time for class. Normally an attendant approached a master's door, gently knocked, waited for a response, and then quietly and mindfully opened the door and said in the least disturbing and most respectful voice possible that it was time for class.

But with Master Renjun, when I arrived at his room fifteen minutes early, and he was inevitably ready, standing outside his door, waiting. He glared at me. I didn't dare say a word.

Renjun's students lived in constant fear of his explosions and rebukes. In class he was very sharp. If the class was scheduled to start at 8:00 a.m., he began at 8:00 on the dot. Not one *second* before or after. If class was scheduled to end at 9:00 that was exactly when he finished. He demanded the same precision from us. If we were allotted five minutes for a presentation, we had to stop at exactly five minutes. If we were late by even an instant, or didn't completely fill our allotted time, he'd shout at us. He had been known to hurl the small clock he kept on his desk at other teachers if they didn't exactly adhere to the schedule.

There was dead silence in the room when he lectured. We sat as still as mummies except for our heads, which enthusiastically bobbed up and down although most of the time we had absolutely no idea what he was talking about. He emphasized every word when he lectured, singing each syllable in his incomprehensible accent, dramatically gesticulating with his arms and hands and cocking his already crooked head as though he were in a Chinese opera. He spoke on general Buddhist topics—whatever struck his fancy. He liked to compose impromptu poems, which he made his interpreter copy on the blackboard. He mulled over these verses, turning them over and considering them from different angles. We thought they were dry, awkward, flat.

We couldn't believe the startling change that took place when we saw Renjun around Master Yinshun, his teacher and the institute's founder. He was a completely different person—a little lamb, gentle and bleating.

I was Renjun's attendant twice during the years I was at the institute, and his old-school fierceness and rigor made a deep impression on me.

That first encounter with Renjun at Fu Yan was in 1997. After I graduated, our paths didn't cross again until 2006, when I was abbot of Master Sheng Yen's Dharma Drum Retreat Center in Pine Bush, New York.

Sheng Yen and I went by car to visit Renjun in Lafayette, New Jersey, where he'd established the Bodhi Monastery and a foundation for the translation and propagation of Yinshun's works and ideas. As we approached, I saw that Bodhi was an elaborate facility, beautifully kept up. Before it was taken over by the foundation, it had been a seminary.

Renjun himself was unbelievably transformed. He greeted me with a big smile—and kept smiling. He was extremely friendly and seemed jolly and mild. What had happened to Hair Stands on End and Shiver Down the Spine?

Renjun confided in me, of all things! He told me that he realized he'd been too strict and stern. He had no students and hadn't ordained anyone. As a result, he had changed his practice to smiling. He spent one hour each day in front of the mirror, smiling at himself. At first, he said, he had actually practiced pulling up the corners of his mouth with his fingers, so ingrained was his ferocious frown.

I was deeply moved, and so was the rest of the Buddhist community when they heard about the newly benevolent Renjun. He was over eighty when he changed his practice and character. We admired and revered him.

My last image of Renjun is peculiar. I saw him walking in and out of the main hall of Bodhi Monastery. I stood back and watched as he removed his shoes, placed them carefully and exactly to one side, went into the hall, came back out, put back on his shoes, and then went through the same process again. I thought that maybe he was a bit unstable. Perhaps he had obsessive-compulsive disorder?

But my curiosity got the better of me, and I went over and asked him what he was doing.

He told me that he had forgotten to take off his shoes before he entered the hall, so now he was practicing. One hundred times, taking off his shoes, entering the hall, and then putting them back on again. It was part of his character: when he made a small mistake, he always corrected himself on the spot.

I was deeply touched, as well as ashamed of all the small things I had let go, considering them unimportant. To this man there was no small thing. It was all part of the whole and the art of living. I left him going in and out of the main hall, smiling and putting on and then taking off his shoes.

The Buddha said that even a small *drip-drip-drip* can fill a large vat with water. No good deed is so small it is not worth doing, and even small transgressions of what we know inside ourselves to be right and true are damaging to who we are and who we want to be. We have a saying in Chinese: A small spark of fire in the summer can burn down a whole forest. We can learn from the example of Master Renjun. We can be attentive to everything. As we go about our lives, the kind of attention we bring to small details and tasks can be joyful and smiling. Renjun put on his shoes and took off his shoes, and he was so happy doing it.

Recent research in neuroscience has found that when we smile, even if we're not happy, our brains secrete hormones that will make us happier. So practice smiling:

> Smile when you walk.
> Smile when you sleep.
> Smile at everything you see.
> Smile when you hear.
> Smile when you breathe.
> Carry that smile, and let it integrate into
>   everything you do.
> Let the smile come to you
> like chocolate melting on your tongue.
> Savor the chocolate, don't bite or chew it.
> Let it melt in your mouth, slowly melt.
> Smile.
> The taste comes slowly.
>
> Open your heart and mind.
> Remember the smile.
> Smile when you tidy your bed.
> Smile when you wash yourself up.
> Brushing your teeth, it's difficult to smile;
> Still, have that attitude and joy.
> It's like fermentation;
> inside you things start to ferment
> The smile breaks down barriers,

pulls down walls,
heals deep wounds.
When your mind is cloudy and scattered
return to the smile.
When you feel pressured
return to the smile.
Your smile is a great treasure.

———

We have two abilities that need not be taught. The first is our ability to breathe. The first moment we live, we breathe. The second is to smile—in fact, scientists have recently discovered that the fetus smiles while it floats in the womb. The fetus smiles, floats, and smiles.

Chan masters always ask, "What is your original nature before you are born?"

Our original nature is smiling and floating.

Before you were born, you were smiling. You can smile to discover your original nature, your primal response to life.

We can return to that state before we were born, floating and smiling in the wombs of our mothers.

Is it so different, floating in this vast universe?

Renjun smiles and takes off his shoes and puts them back on.

Smile and float, cradled in the womb of this great earth.

III.

CHAN HEART,
CHAN MIND

Water dripping ceaselessly
Will fill the four seas.
Specks of dust not wiped away
Will become the five mountains.

Wang Ming,
translated by Master Sheng Yen

17. TALKING SOFTLY

When a couple falls in love they whisper together. They talk softly of their love.

When do we shout? When the person we are trying to reach is far away. We talk softly when that person is near.

Shouting signals you are far from me. We may not realize that when we shout or are shouted at, distance is being unconsciously communicated. *You are far from me.*

When someone shouts at you, go out to that person. Draw near. Talk softly. Be gentle with your words.

Immediately that person will soften.

———

When someone shouts at us, we usually shout back. Then we try to shout louder. As a result, the relationship becomes distant.

We often can't accept being shouted at. We feel shaken or shattered, cold and rejected. We feel distant. When we're close together, we feel warm and connected.

The next time someone shouts at you, listen deeply. That person is calling you, telling you that you are distant. Ask her to tell you what is in her heart. Accept her. To accept means to receive and feel the other person. That will awaken the love and kindness in you.

With love and kindness, you'll come closer. You narrow the distance; you get nearer.

Talk softly as you would to a puppy or a horse; there's no need to shout. Draw nearer. There's enough shouting in the world. Let your words be tender and kind. Like an intimate couple, leaning toward one another, whispering love.

18. BODY AND MIND TOGETHER

I have a mantra that I teach my students: *Wherever the body is, the mind is there; whatever the body is doing, the mind is doing it too.*

Body and mind should be together. When we walk, we just walk. When we sit, we just sit. The body shouldn't be doing something while the mind is wandering off. Body and mind together.

This is not to say that we can't experience deep, meaningful states of absorption when we're in the midst of thought or working out a problem. And there are also meditative states where the external environment drops away and the mind is unified and fully engaged.

Most of the time, however, we're simply living our lives, going about our day-to-day tasks. The mantra helps us to be aware, to keep coming back into the present moment, to not get lost in our emotional states and daydreams and lose ourselves in the stories we generate to explain and justify why we feel this way or that.

The environment in which we live reflects our mental state. Everything is, in fact, a projection of the mind. If the mind is scattered, then our home will have things strewn about: bits and pieces everywhere. We will misplace and lose things.

Since I learned meditation twenty years ago, I don't remember misplacing or losing anything. When I'm traveling I can call my monastery in Singapore if I need something sent to me and tell the person on the phone exactly where it is. I'm not bragging about this ability; it's something very simple, very natural.

Practice returning things to their places. If your room is messy, tidy it up. Don't go about your life in a daze. Body and mind together. If we diligently practice this mantra, we will naturally come back into harmony with our lives. The practice leads us back to the present, to the here and now, to what is real rather than projection and illusion. When body and mind are unified, we are in the moment. Our attention is on what is happening now, and we're fully engaged. Fully alive!

We will naturally enter a very relaxed state if we practice body and mind together. Relaxation is not inertia, however; it's not lax, casual, or careless. Relaxation means not being affected, distracted, or disturbed. It's a state of serene clarity. It's both receptive and responsive.

The Buddha was the most relaxed person in the world. That doesn't mean he was the most *comfortable* person. You can be extremely uncomfortable and still be perfectly relaxed. Relaxation is a state of openness. Nongrasping. Clarity without exertion, force, or pressure.

The flexibility to adapt to each moment. Buddhahood is the perfection of relaxation.

To attain this kind of relaxation, practice the mantra of body and mind together. Wherever the body is, the mind is there. Whatever the body is doing, the mind is doing it too. Very simple. Very easy. Direct and ordinary. Body and mind in unison. Harmony.

Body and mind always together.

19. SEEING BEYOND THE SELF

Chan does not use logic and intellect, although we have nothing against them. Chan is experiential. We stay in the present moment, and we keep returning to it. We are always in process, always in flux, always changing, with no fixed point. In whatever we do, we relax and open our awareness.

If we're relaxed and open, there's a feeling of gentleness. Tenderness. We're naturally moved by a desire to help. We feel connected and compassionate.

The word for "compassion" in Chan is *cibei*. In Chinese, *ci* means "giving happiness." The top part of the character is traditionally translated as "silk," implying softness. The bottom part of the character translates as "heart" or "mind."

We use *cibei* in Chan today to mean "to give happiness and remove suffering." We hope others will be happy, and if possible, we will give them happiness. It means to remove and give. Give and remove.

We cultivate this response to life by always coming back to the present moment. As I've said: wherever the body is, the mind is there; whatever the body is doing, the mind is doing it too. It takes discipline to live like this, yet it is also very relaxed, very easy.

In Chan, we shy from analysis and arguments. Chan is engaged with the intuitive, rather than with what can appear—at least on the surface—as the rational. Take, for example, the meditation retreats I lead. Is it rational to go up into the mountains and sequester oneself for a week or two, waking at 4:00 a.m. and sitting, silent and unmoving, for hours?

When we analyze something, pick it apart, we do it from our own perspective. The fixed point of the self generates our everyday outlook in life. Everything refers to *I*, *me*, *my*. The whole world is about me. A self-referential worldview can produce knowledge, but only knowledge of the self. You see yourself as subject and everything else as object. You think you can manipulate everything, and this leads to hubris.

Our inflated sense of our own importance leads to bloodshed, oppression, and the degradation of nature. It indicates a lack of care, gentleness, kindness, and respect. Its attitude is "I am what's most important. The universe is here to serve *me*!" What misery this creates! And yet if we stop and intuitively attune to the majestic complexity of creation, we can only feel humility and gratitude. Nature keeps giving and giving. Endlessly giving. Every moment is a miracle.

To know this intellectually is one thing. To *feel* it, to

live it, is another. We live our lives unable to see beyond the self, hear beyond the self, have an understanding that is beyond the self. A reality beyond the self is beyond our experience.

Chan calls "knowledge" *zhishi*. "Wisdom" is *zhihui*, which we write by putting the character for the sun below the character for knowledge. The sun shines on everything; wisdom is pervasive. Nonjudgmental. Knowledge, on the other hand, is a narrow beam of light. Its focus and direction are limited.

In Chan, we have an expression: *Ge teng luo suo*. It means our mode of analysis is like a creeping vine, the type of plant that grows up and around a fence. It just goes round and round and in and out of the fence and becomes increasingly entangled. Our reasoning may be subtle and complex, but we're still inexorably attached to the fence. In other words, we are unable to break away from the framework of the self.

A mind consumed by analysis can go crazy. It's like an engine that runs faster and faster. In the end, the engine catches fire and explodes.

Keep coming back to the present moment. Over and over. Body and mind together—walking, talking, eating, drinking. This is how we expand our awareness and manifest compassion even when it seems to defy logic and goes beyond what we can intellectually understand.

20. COURAGE (II)

In Chinese, as in English, there are subtle differences between the concepts of bravery and courage. The word "bravery" derives from *barbaros* in Latin, and it connotes savagery. Chinese is similar: "bravery" means daring and physical prowess. It can be driven by fear. Bravery is expressive; it's about appearances—you may appear "brave" while internally you're not courageous. Courage emanates from the core of our internal energy and from our convictions. Courage is inner strength. It isn't necessarily about physical fighting, although it does imply facing challenges and difficulties directly, with fortitude.

Courage is also a form of tolerance. The strength of courage does not repulse or attack. It withstands. Great courage comes from great compassion. It's like the parent who is always looking after the child, shielding the child, ready to sacrifice himself for the child.

With that kind of compassion, we feel no fear, and we're able to face danger. We need to be able to show this kind of courage to ourselves. If we love the child within us, the child that is innocent and pure, we're able to face difficulties and challenges. Courage comes from love; we need to love ourselves.

Courage comes from wisdom. This kind of courage empowers us to fight for an idea. It was the kind of courage that propelled Mahatma Gandhi and Nelson Mandela to stand up to oppression and injustice and to change the world.

Courage also comes from practice: when we've developed certain skills and practiced them, we have confidence in our expertise. This helps us act decisively, without fear.

Courage comes from loyalty or devotion. All relationships have ups and downs, so willingness to go through hardship and problems depends on courage.

Parents devote themselves to their children. The mother encourages the child: "You can do it!" she says. "Don't give up." The mother believes in the child. This unleashes the child's potential. It inspires the child to make the effort—to be courageous.

Courage is warm. It comes from the heart. So many people today are afraid to communicate with their hearts. They become distant, hard, and cold. That is not the way the mother treats the child. That hard distance is the opposite of courage. It comes from fear.

Courage can also mean to be responsible. To play your part. Irresponsible people are not courageous. They don't want to bear the consequences of their actions. We have a responsibility to ourselves and to each other. To be courageous is to take full responsibility for whatever happens. The Buddha was courageous because he took responsibility for the suffering of mankind.

There is a kind of courage that in Chinese is called *yong*. It has the connotation of going forward, advancing, of diligence and effort. It also means eternity. *Yongmeng* is used to refer to an animal like a lion or tiger that has a fierce and determined energy.

At the end of the day, courage is something that is selfless. Personal gain and loss are put aside. When you're devoted, dedicated, and committed, you don't think. You just do.

Relentless effort is a form of courage. To be unafraid of failure is courageous. It takes courage to venture into the unknown. To be adventurous takes courage. Letting go is a form of courage. Once we let go, we don't know what to hold on to. Relaxing into uncertainty, an uncertain future—that is courage.

21. SELF-RELIANCE

Chan values self-reliance. We Chinese emphasize work and self-sufficiency. There is no tolerance for begging in China. This carries over into Chan: "A day without work is a day without food," Chan Master Baizhang (720–814) famously said. The agrarian foundation of Chinese culture and society, as well as the environment of Chan monasteries until very recently, involved working the land and being self-sufficient by growing your own food.

Self-reliance does not mean going off on your own to live a solitary life disconnected from other people. It means being able to contribute to the group, having something to offer and share. It is the foundation of all caring and responsibility. It emphasizes the responsibility each of us has for his or her own spiritual development.

There is a wonderful Buddhist story that illustrates this point. After the Buddha died, the five hundred *arhats* (enlightened beings) gathered. One disciple, Ananda, was barred from the congregation because he was not yet awakened, although he had been the personal attendant to the Buddha for many years and was renowned for his pure heart and prodigious memory. He was devastated to be excluded from this gathering of his Dharma brothers and sisters so soon after his master's death.

Mahakasyapa, the disciple who had called the gathering, told Ananda to become self-reliant. The word he used in Chinese is *yizhi*: *yi* to follow, to adhere; *zhi*, to stop. Ananda realized he had depended too much on the Buddha and had failed to use his own efforts to develop himself.

Mahakasyapa gave him seven days to awaken and join the congregation. Day and night Ananda practiced all the different types of meditation he knew. Nothing worked. On the evening of the seventh day he was so exhausted and frustrated that he decided it was no use and was about to lie down. At that moment he awakened.

I see Ananda moving downward, toward the earth, finally relaxing, letting go of his fixation on enlightenment. His letting go was not about giving up but about opening, truly opening.

"You are my true teacher," said Ananda to Mahakasyapa. And according to Zen tradition, their lineage continues to this day.

When we feel hopeless and choiceless, it's because we are too dependent and too reliant on others. Our tendency is to project outward, as though what we're searching for is out there. The Buddha is in each of us. Turn inward and recover the Buddha within.

In Chan we call this teaching "the transmission of the lamp." The lamp passes from mind to mind, heart to heart across generations, down through the centuries. The lamp is inside you, waiting to be lit. The room that has been dark for a thousand years is illuminated in an instant by a single light.

22. THE NONESTABLISHMENT
OF WORDS

In Chan, we have a saying that comes from the Lankavatara Sutra: *bu li wen zi*. It means "the nonestablishment of words."

The ninth-century Chan Master Juzhi Yizhi taught in this way, without words. Whenever he was asked a question he would raise one finger. Whatever the question, that was his response.

Yizhi had an attendant who had been with him for many years. For all those years, he saw his master raise one finger whenever he was asked a question.

One day the master was out when a Chan student came to visit. The attendant decided to take his master's place. He tidied himself and sat on the master's seat.

"May I ask a question?" the student asked.

"Go ahead," said the attendant.

In response to the student's question, the attendant raised his finger, just as he had seen his master do. The student went away.

"Did anything happen while I was gone?" the master asked when he returned.

"Someone came," said the attendant.

"Too bad I wasn't around."

"Don't worry. I took your place."

"What did you do?"

The attendant raised his finger. The master leapt up, grabbed a knife—and cut off the attendant's finger! The attendant shouted and jumped to his feet. As he began to run from the room, the master called to him. The attendant turned—and the master again raised his finger. In that moment, the young man awakened.

Is enlightenment worth the loss of a finger? What do you think?

Although Sheng Yen wrote more than one hundred books and valued the power and importance of words, he did not establish himself in words alone. He also embodied the simple, gentle beauty of Chan practice, which was the center of his life.

He described the nonestablishment of words beautifully. He wrote: "Chan is inexplicable because we cannot express, describe, or explain it with words, nor can we imagine it or grasp it with our conceptual mind. Anything that we can express in language, no matter how wonderful, is not Chan."

23. TONGUE OF THE BUDDHA

There is a Chan saying: *Xi sheng jin shi guang chang she.*
It's difficult to translate, but it means something like "the
sound of the river is like the tongue of the Buddha."

The tongue of the Buddha is long. The teachings
spread, going here and there, coming down from their
source as mountain springs, flowing across the land.
Always moving. Always changing. Nothing fixed. The
sound of the river is the Buddha teaching us here and
now.

Nature's beauty is everywhere. In the mountains of
Java where I am now, I look at green hillsides, glistening
fronds of palm and banana, yellow hummingbirds hov-
ering over the lips of flowers, the river pounding in the
gorge below. Thunder booms over the ridge tops. The
wind kicks up. The first fat raindrops explode against the
roof and deck. Soon the rain is roaring. The river plunges
through the valley, sweeping around gray stones. It's so
alive, so vital. It sings to us, ceaselessly teaching us—if
we listen.

If we can appreciate the magnificence of nature, why is
it that we don't equally appreciate human beings? We can
admire each and every flower. Why can't we admire each

and every person? The person you ignore; the person you detest; the person you find distasteful; the person who alienates you; the person who hurts you; the person you desire; the person who has helped you; the person who betrays you; the person you have no use for; the person who seems neutral; the countless people you have never met; the person you will meet tomorrow.

Every person, every person, *every* person—every person is the first person and the last person. Each person is our teacher. Each person is a world, a universe, the Buddha's tongue, a gift, a song, an awakening. Come back to the moment. Come back to the person. Open yourself. Listen!

We eat grass and drink raindrops. Clouds part, revealing the wave-like peaks. The sky grows dark again, and the heavy rain resumes. It seems as though it will never end. Steep hillsides funnel runoff into the ravine below. The river swells.

Buddha's tongue is long. It is always speaking, always teaching, always opening us to the miracle of life, whispering to us with each breath to cherish everything that lives.

24. REPENTANCE

(1)

Repentance practices are central to Chan and have long been a large part of my religious life. They address areas inside us that we don't necessarily understand but are troubled by nonetheless. Repentance practices have given me strength and courage, and they have helped me open up and expand my heart and mind.

I began doing repentance practices when I was only fourteen at the Bright Hill Temple in Singapore. On the twenty-seventh of each month, in accordance with the lunar calendar, we would repent in front of Avalokiteshvara, the bodhisattva of compassion, who is conceived as having a thousand arms weaving from his torso, palms facing outward, each containing a single eye. At Bright Hill, the statue did not quite have a thousand arms, but it had many, and it was huge, over twenty feet high with a wing span of almost that much across. It was made of white Italian marble and was mounted on massive pedestal that was rimmed with pod-like red lights, the kind you might see in a nuclear submarine, a futuristic nightclub, or a spaceship. It had obviously cost a fortune.

Needless to say, this stunning rendition of the bodhi-sattva captured the imagination of a fourteen-year-old boy. It was an impressive figure clearly designed to accomplish great deeds, perhaps even work miracles. The reason the bodhisattva has a thousand arms and eyes are that two are not nearly enough to save all sentient beings; he needs more to do the work.

Standing before the bodhisattva, we did prostrations, first acknowledging all the harmful things we had done and then vowing to help others. As a group, we sang the ten great vows together in a slow, sonorous, trance-inducing voice:

> Praise to infinitely compassionate Avalokiteshvara,
>   may I soon understand all dharmas;
> Praise to infinitely compassionate Avalokiteshvara,
>   may I quickly have eyes of wisdom;
> Praise to infinitely compassionate Avalokiteshvara,
>   may I soon deliver all sentient beings;
> Praise to infinitely compassionate Avalokiteshvara,
>   may I quickly master limitless approaches and
>   skillful means;
> Praise to infinitely compassionate Avalokiteshvara,
>   may I soon be able to sail on the boat of wisdom;
> Praise to infinitely compassionate Avalokiteshvara,
>   may I be able to quickly transcend the ocean
>   of suffering;

Praise to infinitely compassionate Avalokiteshvara,
  may I be able to soon walk the path of shila and
  samadhi;
Praise to infinitely compassionate Avalokiteshvara,
  may I quickly ascend the mountain of nirvana;
Praise to infinitely compassionate Avalokiteshvara,
  may I soon master the perfection of equanimity
  and nonattachment;
Praise to infinitely compassionate Avalokiteshvara,
  may I quickly attain the dharmakaya, the Buddha
  state of all things coming together, nonduality.

The vows were sung very slowly. A ringing chime accompanied them, setting the rhythm. The pace slowly accelerated. The chanting was like an ocean of sound, wave upon wave. We continued chanting:

When I face the mountain of swords and spears,
  they will break.
When I face the ocean of boiling oil, it will dry up.
When I face hell, it will disappear.
The moment I face hungry ghosts, they will be
  fulfilled.
When I face the asuras—anger, jealousy—they will
  disappear.
When I face the animals, they will be attain great
  wisdom.

We called out to Avalokiteshvara ten times, slowing the words during the last iteration, and then we recited the Sanskrit mantra *The Great Compassion Dharani*. There was no need to know the meaning of the words. A great feeling of compassion welled up inside us. It opened our hearts and minds. People wept. It was as if there were a clearing up of everything that was troubling us. We dove into the ocean of compassion. The ritual was shamanic, evangelical, revivalist. It was almost like speaking in tongues. You were infused with spirit. Hundreds of people sang together. We did the mantra many, many times, circulating through the building, putting the vow of great compassion into motion.

This was my repentance practice when I was young.

(2)

I continued on with repentance practices when I was at Mahabodhi with Songnian. He had me do three hundred prostrations to Avalokiteshvara each day. I stood in front of an altar, head bowed, palms together, reciting the name of the bodhisattva, apologizing for past wrongs and hurts, direct and indirect, vowing not to repeat such actions, words, or thoughts, and vowing to help all sentient beings.

I would do my repentance practice whenever I had time, often at night after Songnian had gone to his room. Three hundred prostrations in two hours is quite a workout. I dripped with sweat. It was a cleansing process; it felt like a venting—a discharge and release of all my negativity. After I was done I was refreshed both physically and mentally, as though an internal reevaluation and reconciliation had occurred.

(3)

"Repentance" in Chinese is *chanhui*. *Chan* here doesn't refer to the religion; it means striving forward, the feeling you have let yourself and others down, that there is room for improvement and that we need to strive to reach our full potential. *Hui* means transcending or crossing over.

In Buddhism, repentance can be very personal. You often must apologize to the person you have wronged.

When I lived in Australia, I had a Taiwanese student who had a terrible relationship with her mother. They were always fighting and hurting each other's feelings. My student was an only child. When she was young, her father had left the family and run off with another woman. The mother, perhaps to compensate for the lack of a father in the girl's life, had become extremely controlling. She told her daughter what to wear, what to eat and drink, which friends she was allowed to see and which were forbidden to her, when she needed to be home and when she needed to go out, which boys she should date and not date, and what she should study in school.

On and on—the ways in which the mother sought to control the daughter were endless. As the daughter grew up and became her own person, she chafed at her mother's constant nagging. They ended up in screaming battles nearly each and every day, reducing each other to tears.

Nag, nag, nag.

Yell, yell, yell.

Fight, fight, fight!

Then the mother became gravely ill. But even when she was in the hospital there was no forgiveness on either side. No reconciliation. They fought and fought until the bitter end.

After the mother died, the daughter was consumed by sorrow and guilt. She couldn't focus on meditation.

I suggested that she go to her mother's grave. "Tell her that you are sorry for what you have done and that you love her," I advised. "Prostrate. Lie down on the earth with your whole body. Place your head and hands against the earth. Kiss the earth. Hug the tombstone. If there's a picture on the stone, kiss the picture. Try to make up. First, forgive yourself. Say you're sorry to yourself for all the ways in which you harmed yourself by not being more compassionate and loving. Awaken a feeling of love and forgiveness in your heart. Then forgive her. After you have done this, treat everyone like your mother. Let the love you feel for her manifest in your action and your speech."

My student wept during the interview and then went and did as I suggested, weeping over her mother's grave. After this cathartic event, she felt renewed. She had repented and crossed over and was able to start afresh.

It takes courage to repent, to be able to truly face yourself and to take responsibility for the damage you have done. Repentance involves bearing the full consequences of your actions. Facing your very human imperfections and shortcomings.

(4)

As was true in the case of my student, repentance often involves facing up to our anger. When we become angry and harm someone, most of us are eventually sorry for what we have done. We repent by generating love and compassion for the person we have hurt.

Anger erupts like a volcano, spewing lava everywhere, scalding everyone in its path. It burns and scars. When we are angry, our words are angry. Our actions are angry. At the end of the eruption, when our anger subsides, we feel remorse. *Why did I get so angry? Why did I say what I said? I couldn't help myself!*

When our hearts are full of anger, we injure ourselves as well as others. Renounce the anger; give it up. Generate love and compassion for yourself.

Then, generate that same love and compassion for the person who harmed you. That person acted out ignorance or is overwhelmed by greed, desire, and craving.

We are so helpless. So pitiful. We're all pushed and pulled by our ignorance, greed, craving, impulses, preferences, jealousy, envy—the list is endless! So many traits that torture us. We're lost in a sea of wanderings and scattered thoughts, tormented by aversion and desire.

With this awareness of just how pitiful we are comes humility and forgiveness. This is also one of the forms repentance takes. Forgive yourself and you learn to forgive others.

(5)

We repent in front of the Buddha, a focal point that helps us center and return to ourselves. The Buddha is a source of love and strength, a lens that directs and maintains our awareness. The Buddha focuses and inspires us, and reminds us that there is a buddha within each of us. The Buddha provides refuge.

The word "refuge," or *guiyi*, is central to Buddhism. *Gui* is to turn around and become white. No matter how tainted and impure we are, we can turn around and start fresh. The moment the child turns around and faces the parent and apologizes for what he has done, the parent forgives him.

Turn around and see yourself. You are the true refuge. Look inward to the buddha within.

Yi means to follow, as in following a map or following footsteps. We Chinese don't like to complain. We attempt to resolve problems with inner work; we reflect. We follow the steps to refuge.

Both repentance and refuge bring us to a place of safety and shelter. They bring us back to our original nature, a place of clearness and safety where we can be completely ourselves, filled with innate joy, free to express the best in ourselves without fear, self-consciousness, or self-interest.

When we prostrate in front of the Buddha we embody renunciation, humility. We give everything up. We repent. We take responsibility. We transform anger and hatred into love and compassion. We take refuge. And then a new life begins.

25. LOYALTY

There was once a wealthy old man with four wives. On his deathbed, the man summoned his fourth and youngest wife.

"I have doted on you, given you everything money could buy," he said. "You have been the joy of my old age. Now that I am leaving this world, will you come with me?"

The pretty young wife looked at him with distant pity. "Forgive me, but I want to enjoy life. I'm still so young!"

The old man summoned his third wife. She had been one of his servants when she caught his eye. "I risked my reputation and raised you up from nothing. Now that I'm leaving, will you follow me into the next world?" he asked.

"We had some good times together, and I'm grateful to you," she replied, taking his hand in hers. "You have given me a better life than I could have expected, and I'm afraid I intend to continue to enjoy it."

The old man called for wife number two. It was remarkable how little she had aged. She was still a vigorous woman with a sheaf of shining black hair. How many children had she given him? In his precarious state he couldn't recall. It had been many years since they had been intimate.

"Do you remember when we met?" he said. "I was still a strong young man. We've had many good years together. I provided you with a life of luxury and ease. Now that I'm passing on, will you come along with me?"

She laughed. "Don't you know that for many years I've been in love with Li Pang, our neighbor down the street? I'm sorry, but after you die I'll be free, and I intend to marry him."

The old man called his first wife to him but nodded off before she came. When he awoke, she was sitting next to him on the bed. He could see the quiet, composed, proper young woman she'd once been behind her lined face and gray hair. Theirs had been an arranged marriage and occurred when they were very young.

"Bride of my youth," said the old man. "We have been together these many years. Soon I will be gone. Will you follow me when I go?"

She considered. "You have not been loyal to me. I managed the household for you," she finally said. "Yet you never appreciated the work I did to give you a comfortable home. You spent our resources intemperately, took me for granted, and went with other wives. Nonetheless, I've learned to accept my life as first wife and matriarch of this house. Now you have come back to me at the end. I have been loyal and devoted, and I will continue to be so. I will continue to stay with you, never abandoning you, even in death."

What is the moral of the story?

In the mind of Chan, the youngest wife represents friends who will stand by you when things are going well and share in your good fortune. When hard times come, they desert you.

The third wife, the former servant, symbolizes wealth: your material possessions that will soon be enjoyed by someone else.

The second wife embodies knowledge, power, and status—your position in life. All these will be taken over by someone else when you die.

The loyal first wife is your breath and the present moment, which are always there for you, even if you stray and take them for granted again and again and again.

26. TAKING FOR GRANTED

We take so much for granted.

Cover your nose and mouth with your hand. You quickly feel as though you're suffocating. Do we have to wait until we can't breathe to truly appreciate and value our breath? The breath is so important, so wonderful, so good! We are so lucky to be able to breathe.

It's not only our breath that we take for granted. Only when we're about to lose people—or after we have lost them—do we realize how much they mean to us. How often do we remember them with feelings of longing and regret?

Please do not take your life for granted. Make good use of every opportunity; make good use of each moment. Cherish every breath, and reflect on the preciousness of this human life. Stay in the present moment—each one is beyond price. When this moment goes, will it come back again? Treasure each and every breath.

27. WARM YOURSELF UP!

The root and cause of mind is a raw and naked place.

The experience of this state is a station on our inward journey as we move into deep meditation. In Chan, we call it the changing point, the melting point, the starting point, the point of transformation. You reach that original place where everything drops off, and then you go a step further. And in that state, you see the raw and naked you.

You're as defenseless as a newborn baby; you can't fend for yourself. There is fear—great fear. The ego can no longer hide. You want to put on cloths and cover yourself. There's nothing to hold on to here; it's like trying to stand on space. The nature of impermanence is all too real, too apparent—a wound that is very fresh, very sensitive.

When you come to the melting place, you lose yourself. It's as though you're in a strange country and you've lost your wallet, passport, money, keys, and clothes. You can't speak the language, and you're in a strange, threatening place, in the middle of nowhere, far from anyone you know and love. You're cold, naked, and alone. You must make friends and warm yourself up!

The Buddha said that we need to become a friend to ourselves: a friend that comes uninvited, with no conditions, with total acceptance. When there's nothing to hold on to, when we feel alienated, isolated, and lonely, the Buddha said to generate this friendliness. This friend who comes unasked knows you're in trouble; that friend doesn't need to be invited. Such a friend comes to your aid, to help you and give comfort.

Be friendly; embrace your life. Be kind to yourself. Forgive yourself. Accept yourself totally. Become your own friend. Welcome yourself in. Accept yourself without conditions. Without bias or judgments—with melting, life-giving warmth.

28. ALL AROUND US, ALL THE TIME

We're always moving from one point to another, in constant transition, constant flux. We lie down to sleep and get up when we awaken. We sit, stand, walk, stretch, raise a cup to our lips, drink, and put the cup down. We experience constant change from one moment to the next. It is ongoing and relentless.

We sustain ourselves through the food we eat and air we breathe. What goes in, must come out. We inhale but can that breath stay inside us? We eat and then what? In order to live there must be constant change. Constant movement.

We cannot be still. We cannot hold on to anything. What courage that takes!

The Buddha's teaching of impermanence is always with us, in the air we breathe and food we eat. It's as close as the wind that rustles the leaves, moving past us, hurrying where? Our planet journeys round the sun, and the sun sails across the sky. The moon is new, then full, and disappears into the whirling stars. We never leave the teachings. We never deviate from them. They are inexhaustible. And yet we are always searching for them, even when they are everywhere, in everything, all around us, all the time.

29. SKY POEM (II)

So much openness
in this ancestor teaching
transmission of lineage masters
sky space
so vast and boundless

Thunderstorms, fighter jets
planets and galaxies
the sky unmoving
undisturbed
quietly there

Nothing hinders
nothing attaches
nothing stays
free, still, and silent
thunder roars
birds chirp
airplanes soar

All encompassing
all embracing

cannot be cut or shattered
completely open
undisturbed
anything can happen
practicing
SILENCE

IV.

ENGAGING WITH
THE WORLD

Tansheng was making tea.
"Who is that tea for?" Daowu asked.
"There is someone who wants it."
"Why doesn't he come himself?"
"Fortunately I'm here to do it."

30. MARA'S ARMIES

Some time ago I was learning how to drive.

"You look so relaxed. Nothing rattles you," the driving coach remarked. It was true. I was relaxed even when I was about to drive us into a tree! Fortunately, I pressed the brakes in time.

The coach was terrified.

I looked at him and smiled. "Sorry," I said.

"How can you remain so calm? We nearly crashed!"

"It's the meditation. You should tell all your driving students to meditate."

Our lives are like that. We usually know what to do when we're in danger or face difficulties—press the brakes to avoid a crash! So why get frightened? When a problem arises, just solve the problem. We exhaust ourselves with a lot of unnecessary worry.

In Chan training we have a practice called Fast Running Meditation. The master screams, shouts, kicks, hits, and chases you as you sprint around the Chan hall.

These masters can be brutal. "Faster! Faster! Faster!" they shout. You don't react. You just do it. You respond by running faster. The master smacks you. You don't become scared or distracted. You just run. You just run faster. You leave everything behind you. If he chases you, you just increase your pace. Faster and faster. You don't carry anything with you. You don't take anything along. In order to go faster, you drop everything. Right and wrong. Good and bad. Why me? When will it end? Why is this happening? I can't do it! How unfair! Too much pain. All of it. You just drop it. Leave it behind. Put it down. Nothing holds you. It's like running with a herd of wild animals. Some drop out, collapsing on the side. You pay no attention. You gallop along. People gasp for air, panting. Some crumple. You jump over them like jumping over a river. You relax body and mind even as you sprint at full speed. You're sweating. The sweat pours off you. You're running under the blazing sun. The howling wind is your breath. The rain is your sweat. You just keep running. Faster and faster. The masters smack and beat you. You just do it. You go fast. You go faster. The masters punch you and kick you. You don't give it a moment's thought. You throw down everything you carry. You drop it. You sprint. You fly. Finally, the master slams his stick on the floor. The sound is like a thunderbolt. "STOP!" he shouts. Then stillness. Silence.

That was part of my training. Many of the Chan masters I studied with didn't worry in the least about being gentle or nice. Helping me feel comfortable was the last thing on their minds. They trained me to deal with all kinds of uncomfortable situations.

How often do things go smoothly? Chan teaches us to live with challenges and difficulties.

Mara, king of the demons, knew that Buddha was about to reach enlightenment as he sat under the bodhi tree. Mara came marching with his army of millions. They launched arrows, javelins, and spears. Nothing moved Buddha.

Mara tried another approach. His daughters—beautiful young women—danced for Buddha, shedding their clothes, trying to tempt him. Nothing worked!

Now I appreciate the Chan masters who were so tough on me; they were actually showing great compassion. All the shouts, rebukes, kicks, and punches were acts of love. The real practice of Chan only comes when we face hardship, when we fully engage with the imperfect world and Mara comes with his armies.

Chan is not about sitting on your cushion and feeling blissed out. Chan happens in this world with all its heartache and pressures.

31. OPEN HEART, OPEN MIND

After attaining enlightenment, Master Huineng, the sixth ancestor, ran away from jealous monks who were trying to kill him. He went into hiding, living in the forest with hunters. Huineng couldn't hunt so they put him in the kitchen cooking. Killing animals for food is a breach of the Buddhist precept that forbids doing harm, but what do you think he cooked? Tofu? How did this lineage master of Chan reconcile himself to a way of life that was radically out of line with his vows? How did he live in harmony and friendship with the hunters in what could have been a difficult, uncomfortable situation?

Huineng's choice to live with the hunters represents adaptability, an open-mindedness and flexibility that is at the heart of Chan. Huineng didn't look down on the hunters. He made friends. He became part of the family. He was fully integrated, fully part of that life.

Master Sheng Yen had a similar predicament. He served in the Nationalist army for ten years doing clerical and administrative work. Despite disrobing during this period, he studied Buddhism and wrote Buddhist articles. In his heart he still wanted to be a monk. He turned the situation into an opportunity to learn, a productive period.

Like Master Huineng, I had my own period of "living in the forest" when I was a young monk studying psychology and sociology at Monash University in Melbourne. I purposely wanted to experience life with the hunters, so I decided to live in your typical college dorm.

The kids smoked marijuana, slept around, and partied late into the night. They fell down drunk, passing out in pools of vomit. In the morning, I gingerly stepped over their supine forms. They looked ghastly and smelled putrid. They had been so beautiful and lively the night before!

This environment was a potent reminder to me that we live in samsara. My attitude about their behavior was—that's life!

At first my dorm mates were curious about me and a little bit wary. What was a celibate monk—who didn't drink, take drugs, or eat meat—doing living in their den of iniquity? Had I come to spy or preach or try to convert them?

It took them a little while to trust me. When they realized that I was nonjudgmental, they began to seek me out. My door was always ajar, and they came to me for counseling. I accepted them as they were. I didn't impose my standards or beliefs. I helped them to discover themselves. I was a friend. I never told them what to do, and their behavior never affected the tranquility in my room.

I stayed only one semester in the dorms. It was enough.

After that I moved out and lived with roommates in houses close to campus. I needed to move because I had religious work: Buddhists came to visit me, and the dorms horrified them. The final straw, however, was a visit by my *popo*, my grandmother, during a break in the school year when the students had returned home. My popo was appalled by the rows of empty beer and wine bottles lined up like trophies on every shelf. I guess she expected books! A pornographic magazine lay in full view on a coffee table. She was speechless, and I knew it was time to go.

During this period, I learned to be flexible and open. Like Huineng I learned to adapt. Life is multidimensional. The Buddha doesn't give fixed answers for what is right or wrong, good or bad. Imposing our standards on others will not create a happier, more peaceful world.

We should not limit ourselves because we have expectations about the way life should go or strong opinions about how people should live. In Buddhism, we don't discriminate. We are not judgmental, prejudiced, or self-righteous. We don't put ourselves above others.

There is a Chinese saying: "Although the hands, legs, and arms are different, they are all part of one body and work together." This is very Chan. The right hand holds the hammer and the left holds the nail. If the right accidentally hits the hand, the left does not retaliate and hit the right. Rather it goes to the right to be rubbed, held, and soothed.

We live in samsara. That is precisely where we live. By not acknowledging this we are not making good use of the present moment. Embrace life with all its foibles and delusions. It has never been more important to embrace our differences. Closing our hearts and minds only obscures opportunities to learn and grow. It deadens the liveliness and beauty of this world.

Open heart. Open mind.

32. REACT/RESPOND

We often confuse reacting with responding, which creates all kinds of trouble. In English, the meaning of the two words is somewhat different, but they do not stand in opposition to each other in quite the same way they do in Chinese.

To react is *fanying*, which means to fan a fire, to make the flames jump up. *Fan* means "opposite," and *ying*, as it's written in the Chinese character, means "to resonate." *Fanying* could be thought of as something like Newton's first law: for every action there is an equal and opposite reaction. You shout in the mountain, and the sound comes echoing back. Slap someone in the face, and your palm stings. Spit up into the sky, and it comes back in your face.

To respond, on the other hand, is *ganying*. *Gan* means to feel, to be able to sense, to be in tune. *Ganying* then is to empathize, to attune, to come into alignment with rather than to oppose. It means to feel and to resonate. *Xiangying*, a related word, means to feel together: to meet mind to mind, eye to eye, heart to heart.

We so often react rather than respond. All that does is fan the flames. We run around frantically putting out fires! We push back when we feel pushed. Hurt when we are hurt. Stand in opposition when we want to be close. Shout when we want to be heard. Lash out when we want to be embraced.

When you find yourself reacting, come back into the present moment. Relax your discriminating mind, and rest all the grasping and rejection inside of you that says, "I am over here, and you are over there," "I am right, and you are wrong."

Let others reach you. Resonate with them. Breathe with them. Be with them. Respond.

33. WE GIVE MEANING
TO OUR LIVES

When I was living in New York, homeless people often approached me on the street, asking for money. The Mahayana vow I took to remove suffering is very clear: we should try to help people whenever possible. Yet what if the homeless person bought drugs or alcohol with what I gave him? In the long term, at least, that could only add to his suffering.

Chan distinguishes between wants and needs. Drugs and alcohol are not essential to our lives (no matter what some people might tell you). We always try to help with what people need, but what they want is another issue.

"What do you need money for?" I asked.

"I haven't eaten today, I'm hungry," was often the response.

"I can't give you money. But, if you'd like, I will buy you something to eat."

I was frequently taken up on this offer, and I'd find myself having coffee and doughnuts with someone who was living a very hard life.

"Would you like another doughnut?" I'd ask.

In Chan, we don't sympathize; we empathize. Sympathy implies separation, condescension, and pity. We put ourselves up here and other people down there. We say that our lives are somehow better than theirs. Chan doesn't distinguish between our life and that other life. It is all one life, one experience, one whole. We feel the suffering in the world. We empathize. And we want to help.

Accounts I have read of the atrocities in the Congo move me to tears. The story of Masika particularly impressed me and made me vow to go to Africa one day to try to generate kindness and peace.

Masika lived in area caught in the crosshairs of war. Soldiers broke into her home, where she and her family were hiding. They cut up her husband in front of her and made her eat his flesh and then raped her on top of his dismembered body parts. They also raped her two young daughters.

Masika burned with a desire for vengeance. Her suffering was so intense that she understandably thought of suicide. Yet she slowly transformed. She realized that many other women in the Congo were in the same predicament: raped, their husbands and children slaughtered, their homes burned to the ground, left with absolutely nothing.

Masika's suffering gave rise to compassion, and she started a support group for women who had endured, as she had, the horrors of war.

Masika is an extreme example. Not all of us can attain such saint-like forgiveness and compassion. But we can do our best.

Much to the distress of his followers, Sheng Yen refused the kidney transplant that would probably have prolonged his life, insisting that available kidneys go to younger people.

We can always choose to be compassionate.

What is the source of the strength Masika found to go on living?

Buddhism seeks to transform experience. This is its fundamental aim. That is what the Buddha was after when he saw all the suffering in the world and developed Buddhism to help people overcome it. That is why Chan Master Yunmen said, "Every moment is a good moment. Every day is a good day. Every opportunity is a good opportunity."

An opportunity to do what? To transform our experience, to open ourselves, to come back to the present moment. To give rise to awareness, love, kindness, forgiveness, and compassion.

We give meaning to our lives. Happiness or sorrow—it's up to you. You define it. You write your own story. No one writes it for you.

34. YOU'VE ALREADY GOT IT!

We have to work hard. Anything worth attaining takes effort. It doesn't happen by itself.

Our modern world has turned its back on the value of patience. We have lost the virtue of diligence. My students want instant enlightenment. The more you want it, the more elusive it is. Perhaps it's a comforting paradox that each time you realize you can't get it, you've already got it!

That's the way our minds work. Each time we notice our impatience, we can develop patience. When we realize that we're not putting forth good effort, we can become diligent. Recognizing that we lack compassion can create compassion.

When we realize that we have created distance, we can become closer. When we know we've created enmity, we can start to create friendship. When we realize we've lost touch, we can start turning toward one another. When we feel we've let others down—at that moment we can begin to make up.

Asking why we are unable to do it is the beginning of wisdom. When we realize we've lost it, we've actually got it. When we feel happy that we're doing it, we're already starting to lose it! And when you realize you've got it, it's already gone.

35. LEARNING TO FEEL

We're always asked, "How are you? How do you feel today?" We may respond that we're feeling fine or have a headache or are in a good mood or bad mood, or that we're sad because our dog just died or concerned because our child is having trouble in school or overwhelmed because someone close to us is ill.

Day by day, week in and week out, we exist in these mental states and confuse them with feeling, really feeling, until we no longer know how to really feel.

Do you feel yourself? Do you feel yourself seeing, hearing, touching? Do you feel the sound of your voice? Do you feel your breath? Do you feel your blood flowing? Your eyes moving? Your brain processing the words on this page? Do you feel the subtle, almost imperceptible movements of your body?

When you're walking outside, do you feel the sun? Do you feel the air against your face? Do you feel the ground on which you're walking? Are you connected with and aware of the environment? Or are you engrossed in your own emotional state? Busy with all your wandering and scattered thoughts?

Come back to the present moment. Feel your life!

This is your birthright. It's why we were born. Open up. When you walk, feel the ground beneath your feet. Feel the air you breathe entering your nostrils, moving down through your throat, and filling your lungs. Feel the breeze against your skin and the warm sun.

Without this kind of awareness, our lives quickly fade into dullness. They become monotonous. Tasteless. The present moment and the breath connect us to the world. With them, we feel the excitement of being alive. We open to life's potential and possibilities. Each moment is sacred and special. We want to help, to serve. When we truly feel, we feel intimate with all that is.

36. HUGGING A MONK

In Chinese, we use the word *wu zhuo*, which means "nonattachment," rather than the English word "detachment" to describe the state of lively awareness we cultivate in Chan. To detach in English means to disengage and disconnect. It implies being at a remove, even apathetic or aloof. This is not at all what Chan means by nonattachment. "Nonattached" in Chinese means to be untainted. The word connotes clarity, freedom, and aliveness. It's a creative state.

There's a Chan parable that teaches us about the difference between detachment and nonattachment:

A woman who was a devoted Chan practitioner had a pretty young daughter. Each day the mother gave the daughter food to take to a monk who was on a solitary retreat in a hut the family owned in the mountains. The mother wanted to support the monk in his spiritual development.

One morning before the daughter set out for the hut the mother told her: "After you give the food to the monk, try to hug him."

When the daughter returned home, she told her mother, "I hugged the monk."

The next day the mother went up to the hut. "What happened yesterday?" she asked.

"I meditated," said the monk.

"What else?"

"Your daughter brought me food."

"And then?"

"She hugged me."

"How did it feel?"

"A withered branch clings to a cold cliff," the monk replied.

"I've been feeding a rock!" the mother exclaimed. She chased away the monk with a broom. Then she burned down the hut.

What angered the mother? Why did she chase away the monk and raze the hut?

The monk was obviously hardworking and in a state of renunciation. He had detached from the world and left this life. He had left it all behind. To him the pretty young daughter is a withered branch. He is a rock—a cold rock. There is no reaction between them.

Is this reality?

No.

What is real?

Chan is about being aware. To be aware is to be more alive. Awareness in Chan is about living fully in the present moment.

When someone hugs you, what do you feel? At the very least, you sense the pressure and heat of that person's body. It's very simple: two bodies come together, and there is warmth.

The burning hut is a pointer—a street sign that points the way to truth, to realization. In this case, the pointer is directing us away from what is forced and contrived. It's telling us to not make ourselves too complex!

The monk's state is not in the here and the now. He is in another place. He is caught in the trap of thinking that practice is about living in another dimension. That is a fantasy. A trance. A false world generated out of fear of what is real.

We freeze ourselves to shun our own impermanence and the ceaseless flux of our lives. We become fixated on fantasies and dreams. Perhaps this is done with good intentions, even noble aspirations. But no matter how exulted our motives, such strategies for spiritual development have nothing to do with Chan. Chan is what is real in the here and now. It's concrete and natural, simple and ordinary.

I had my own hugging-the-monk experience when I was on retreat in Seoul. A young woman came to the monastery quite often. It was impossible not to notice her; she was as pretty as a movie star!

One day, when I wasn't expecting it, she came up and hugged me.

"*Sarang heyo*, Sunim!" she said in Korean. I had been studying the language and knew that "*Sara heyo*" means "I love you" and "Sunim," an honorific, means "Venerable."

I smiled. "I love you, too!" I said. "But I love all sentient beings more." She began to cry, and I patted her shoulder.

I don't regret this decision or my decision, generally, to forgo these kinds of attachments. I don't like to be restricted, and I don't want to devote myself to only one or two people. My commitment is to serve humanity.

When you practice you become more awake and alive. Not only to yourself but the world at large. The monk needs to wake up and not let girl's desire or his own limit his awareness.

The world vibrates with the awareness of all sentient beings. You can sense their situation, their struggles, hopes, needs, and desires. How lost we all are, and how beautiful and precious.

We need to keep coming back to the present moment. Spiritual maturity is so often obscured by dogma. Return to the here and now. Return to your own experience. Don't confuse detachment and nonattachment. Take your broom. Sweep out what is cold and stale. Then burn your hut.

37. ENGAGING WITH THE WORLD

Before Songnian died, he said that he wanted to rebuild Mahabodhi Monastery and expand it. He had plans drawn up and told the architects that he would sit at the construction site and supervise the building process. Who can guess what they thought about that! Songnian wanted to rebuild Mahabodhi as a seminary. At that time, there wasn't such a place in Singapore. Monks had to go abroad to study Buddhism.

In 2009 the opportunity arose to fulfill Songnian's last wish and begin this project. I was approached by a group of businessmen who offered me money and support. This group pressed me to start the project quickly; they said that later on they would be too old and wouldn't have the same money, influence, and connections. They assured me that they would be fully responsible.

It was clear that they were financially capable when they donated the project's seed money—about $1.5 million, ten percent of the total anticipated cost. They began to raise funds. We hired an architect, and I flew between Singapore and Sydney for meetings. There were endless Skype sessions at all hours.

I looked through more than two hundred books on architectural design. I wanted a building that would be modern and traditional, tasteful and functional. The design should embody the teachings and meaning of Chan and Chinese Buddhism. I wanted something modern and eco-friendly to indicate that we were bringing Buddhism into the twenty-first century.

Everything proceeded as planned. The old, dilapidated monastery building was demolished, and I went with the monks and nuns under my charge into temporary housing.

Then something interesting happened. The funders brought me to a meeting of their so-called "brothers." The meeting took place at night, at a restaurant. I brought my vice abbot. He was aghast! There were cartons of Marlboro and Dunhill cigarettes, which they insisted were ruinously expensive, and everyone was smoking. They were gorging themselves on meat, whole fish, and huge prawns. My vice abbot couldn't believe his eyes. They had a vegetarian meal prepared for us, and although he loves to eat, my vice abbot barely touched his food. "Relax," I told him. "It's okay. No big deal." He was particularly unsettled when they animatedly explained the different types of hard liquor on display. They cracked open bottles at a great rate. Soon everyone was roaring drunk and the table next to ours exploded into drunken song. Not at all Buddhist, I thought. But as long as their hearts were good, and they wanted to do good deeds, I thought that I should give them a chance.

I remembered the Chan parable about a monk who created lots of problems in his monastery. He got into fights and was greedy, always eating more than his share. He was lazy, skipping out of chores, letting others do his work. He was messy and never picked up after himself. He talked about the other monks behind their backs and said nasty things about them that weren't true. He liked to pretend he was sick when he wasn't. In short, he was a pain in the neck.

The other monks finally had enough. They went to their master: "We can't take it anymore. Either he goes or we go," they said.

"I'll keep him," the master replied.

They were stunned. "Why?" they shouted in unison.

The master was gentle and composed. "All of you will survive. You will get by in the world. If he goes, what will he do? He'll have nowhere to go. He may not survive, because he can't get along. What will happen to him?"

The monks softened at their master's words.

Like the master in the story, I reminded myself that I shouldn't judge people by their actions. The businessmen and their way of behaving may have been all that they had been exposed to. If we are judgmental and disassociate from such situations, people who might benefit from the teachings most will never have an opportunity to learn and grow. I wanted to meet these businessmen on their own terms and on their own turf. I wanted to speak to them in their own language and connect with them on their own frequency. That is the bodhisattva path: to go where one is most needed and can do the most good.

Some people had cautioned me about the reputation of these businessmen, but it was only after the initial excavation of the new monastery building that I began to realize the funders and I had profound differences in style and approach. When our architectural and consulting team rejected the contractors they wanted, they resigned from the board and demanded that I return their original donation.

That was impossible. It was not my money! It belonged the monastery's public building project fund. A donation is a donation and a gift is a gift; according to Singapore law, donors can only ask for a refund when their money is used for other than purported purposes. This was clearly not the case.

Strange troubles began. Four different attorneys sent four different letters, each one promising legal action if the monastery didn't refund the money in seven days. Rumors circulated that I was going to jail. My students were beside themselves.

Then I was called to come into the central police headquarters to assist the police with an investigation. I went with my lawyer and auditor, but the authorities didn't want to talk to them, only to me, and they sat waiting while I went through what turned out to be a ten-hour interrogation. When they had heard every detail of my life story and were finally satisfied that I had done nothing wrong, they released me, and a week later I received a letter from the attorney general saying the case was closed.

You might think that would have been the end of it. Unfortunately, no. Soon after the attorney general's letter came, false claims against me began to appear. Letters from someone claiming to have discovered emails between me and my supposed "boyfriend" appeared on websites and arrived at every monastery in Singapore. Rumors circulated that when I went out of Singapore to lead retreats and give lectures I would be killed.

My students were understandably very upset. Our old temple had been demolished, our new temple was going to cost $15 million, which we didn't have, and the upcoming legal battle promised to be expensive. It felt to them as though the sky were falling.

The only thing I could do was relax. When students came to me with questions, in a panic, I told them: Don't worry, it's okay, no big deal, relax.

The Buddha said when a poison arrow hits you, don't think about who shot it or why. Extract the arrow and treat the wound. I told my students that there isn't a single person who is unanimously loved and respected or hated and reviled. Good people do bad things, and we should not judge people by their actions. Sometimes we're in a situation where we're helpless and can't do anything. What we can do is *relax*. Deal with things as they come. Respond rather than react. Keep returning to the present moment. That is what will sustain and support us. When no one trusts you, trust yourself. When no one loves you, love yourself. When no one believes in you, believe in yourself.

The whole episode was like a madly whirling maelstrom. Coming back to the breath and the present moment returned me to the eye of the storm. Everything was calm while all around fierce winds howled.

When everything is okay inside of you, what's happening outside is not such a big issue. Things move and change. Nothing is fixed. Give it time, and there will be change. You don't need to push. Remain calm and steady, and you won't be engulfed. The storm will dwindle or move on.

Mahabodhi Monastery is almost finished and will open soon. I see Songnian in the building's structure and style. I wanted the design of the building to reflect his calligraphy, which is contemporary and advanced, simple and clean in its line. He was extremely attentive to detail, and

I have tried to be too. The structure reflects his strength and stature. It is muscular as well as elegant and refined.

Songnian might have approved of the troubles I have had rebuilding Mahabodhi. He taught me that nothing worthwhile is ever easy. Making ink takes time, energy, patience, and focus. It takes commitment. I suppose I will always hear him scolding me. But I do hope he would be pleased.

ACKNOWLEDGMENTS

My editor, Kenneth Wapner, and I created this book through interviews in Singapore, Vancouver, Hong Kong, and Indonesia based on Dharma talks that had been transcribed by my Chan students.

During the book's development, there were so many things going on. I had surgery for a retina detachment and almost went blind in one eye. This occurred at the same time as the arduous process of trying to finish building Mahabodhi Monastery in Singapore. So the book took form during a long period of extreme pressure. Part of what kept me going was gratitude for my teachers and for the people who were helping me. I didn't want to let them down. I wanted to keep moving forward.

This book is dedicated to Master Yinshun, Master Renjun, and Dad Lai Chok Yau. It is dedicated to all those who made possible the rebuilding of Mahabodhi Monastery. I owe a deep debt of gratitude and thanks to those people who supported me when I had retina detachment surgery and who cared for me during my recuperation. Finally, I wish to give thanks to all the

Chan students who helped transcribe, edit, and proof-read the text.

It is with heartfelt thanks that I dedicate this book to all of you.

Guojun Fashi

EDITOR'S NOTE

This book was built around transcripts from Master Guojun's Dharma talks to his Indonesian and North American sanghas. These materials were supplemented by conversations I had with Master Guojun during retreats he led in Indonesia, British Columbia, and China in 2013 and 2014. My thanks to these sanghas for their support and hospitality. And my thanks always to Shifu for his willingness, patience, and wisdom.

Kenneth Wapner

Woodstock, NY

ABOUT THE AUTHOR

Ven. Guojun was born in Singapore in 1974 and ordained as a monk under Ven. Songnian of Mahabodhi Temple, Singapore. He is one of the youngest Dharma heirs of the renowned Chan master Sheng Yen.

Ven. Guojun has a diploma in biotechnology from Ngee Ann Polytechnic, Singapore. He also earned a degree in Buddhist philosophy from Fu Yan Buddhist Institute, Taiwan, a bachelor of arts in psychology and sociology from Monash University, Australia, and a masters in Buddhist studies from the University of Sydney, Australia.

Ven. Guojun has practiced meditation intensively since 1997. He has studied Tibetan Buddhism and Theravada Buddhism, as well as various aspects of the Mahayana tradition.

Ven. Guojun speaks Mandarin, Korean, and English and has taught around the world. He is also a spiritual and guiding teacher of Chan Community Canada and Dharmajala Indonesia. He was the abbot of Dharma

Drum Retreat Center in Pine Bush, New York, from 2005 to 2008. He is the author of *Essential Chan Buddhism*, which has been published in several languages. He is currently the abbot of Mahabodhi Temple in Singapore.

Zen's Chinese Heritage

The Masters and Their Teachings

Andy Ferguson

Foreword by Reb Anderson and Steven Heine

"This is an indispensable reference for any student of Buddhism. Ferguson has given us an impeccable and very readable translation."
—John Daido Loori, late abbot, Zen Mountain Monastery

Novice to Master

An Ongoing Lesson in the Extent of My Own Stupidity

Sōkō Morinaga

Translated by Belenda Attaway Yamakawa

"This wise and warm book should be read by all."
—Anthony Swofford, author of *Jarhead*

Inside the Grass Hut

Living Shitou's Classic Zen Poem

Ben Connelly

Foreword by Taigen Dan Leighton

"The very essence of Zen."
—Mike O'Connor, translator of *Where the World Does Not Follow*

About Wisdom Publications

Wisdom Publications is the leading publisher of classic and contemporary Buddhist books and practical works on mindfulness. To learn more about us or to explore our other books, please visit our website at wisdompubs.org or contact us at the address below.

Wisdom Publications
199 Elm Street
Somerville, MA 02144 USA

We are a 501(c)(3) organization, and donations in support of our mission are tax deductible.

Wisdom Publications is affiliated with the Foundation for the Preservation of the Mahayana Tradition (FPMT).